THE INDEPENDENT GUIDE TO UNIVERSAL ORLANDO 2024

G. COSTA

GW00467455

Contents

Introduction

In 1971, Orlando was put on the map as the theme park capital of the world with the opening of the *Walt Disney World Resort*. Here families could make memories to last a lifetime.

The *Walt Disney World Resort* was a giant version of the Disneyland Resort that opened in 1955 in Anaheim, California.

In the late 1980s, Universal announced it would open its own East Coast theme park, similar to the one it operated in Hollywood.

Disney saw this new theme park as a significant threat and also started building a theme park based around movie studios.

Miraculously, Disney's park, which was called *MGM Studios* at the time,

managed to open its doors in 1989, before the grand opening of *Universal Studios Florida* one year later. *MGM* was a rushed project, and *Universal Studios Florida* blew Disney's theme park away when it opened the following year in 1990.

In 1995, the expansion of Universal's Orlando project began as the company invested billions of dollars in creating a second theme park, *Universal's Islands of Adventure*. Three on-site resort hotels and an entertainment and dining district, *CityWalk*, were also unveiled.

The original *Universal Studios Florida* park was also expanded with new areas to create a multi-day destination rivaling Disney. In 1999, *Universal's Islands*

of Adventure opened to rave reviews. It featured innovative attractions such as *The Amazing Adventures of Spider-Man* and *The Incredible Hulk Coaster* which win awards year after year, even to this day.

The *Universal Orlando Resort* has fast become *the* must-visit place in Orlando. Innovative attractions and areas such as *The Simpsons Ride* and *The Wizarding World of Harry Potter*, have sent visitor figures sky-rocketing. Collectively, both theme parks now welcome over 22 million guests yearly.

2024 marks an exciting year for the resort as it unveils a new Dreamworks-themed area for younger visitors, and the resort prepares for the addition of a new theme park in 2025.

Tickets

All About Tickets

The easiest place to purchase advanced theme park tickets is the official Universal Orlando website at universalorlando.com. Guests who do not buy their tickets in advance can do so at the theme parks, but prices there are higher. Guests from any country can buy advanced tickets.

Ticket Types:
There are two types of tickets:

• A *Single Park* ticket allows you access to one park per day (either *Universal Studios Florida* or *Islands of Adventure* or *Volcano Bay* on any one day)

• A *Park-to-Park* ticket allows you to enter all the parks on the same day.

Multi-day Single Park tickets allow you to visit different parks on separate days. However, you cannot visit more than one park on a single day (for that you need a *Park-to-Park* ticket).

Tickets vary in price depending on the visit date. Tickets during peak season are more expensive than off-peak tickets.

Single Park tickets allow you to ride every attraction in one single theme park (except the *Hogwarts Express* which requires a *Park-to-Park* ticket).

You can upgrade a *Single Park* ticket to a *Park-to-Park* ticket for an additional fee. You will need to decide if the flexibility of moving

between parks on the same day (and access to the *Hogwarts Express*) is worth the extra cost.

Child prices apply to children aged 3 to 9 years old. Children under 3 get free admission into the theme parks (proof of age may be requested on entry). Prices exclude tax.

Getting your tickets:
Advanced Tickets can be purchased and scanned directly on the Universal Orlando app, printed at home, mailed to you (extra charge), or picked up from 'Will Call' kiosks at the theme park entrances.

Save with advanced tickets:
All multi-day tickets cost $20 less when purchased online than at the parks.

The 'Will Call' kiosks near the park entrances can only be used to pick up advanced tickets. If you have not purchased in advance, you will need to wait in the ticket queue line to see a

Team Member and buy your tickets. Alternatively, you can book on the Universal Orlando app or by phone.

You can also buy tickets at any on-site hotel and save $20 on park prices.

Can I add extra days to my ticket later?
Yes. To add extra days to your park ticket, visit Guest Relations at either park before your last day of admission expires. Here, your tickets can be upgraded for the difference in price. Adding an extra day can be very affordable.

Are there any ways to get discounted tickets?
Ticket brokers may offer tickets at reduced prices. Check the reputation of the site you are purchasing from. Avoid second-hand sales and auction websites. One trusted ticket broker is UndercoverTourist.com. Florida residents can access discounted tickets too - proof of residency is required.

More about Tickets

Can I buy a ticket only for Volcano Bay Water Park?
Yes. A *Volcano Bay Water Park* ticket starts at $80 per adult and $75 per child.

Do international visitors get a discount?
There are special *Universal Explorer* tickets. These are

targeted at visitors from Europe (specifically the UK). The 2024 price for a 14-day 2-Park Explorer Ticket is £345 per adult and £335 per child. A 3-park ticket (with access to *Volcano Bay Water Park*) is the same price as the 2-Park ticket. These tickets are sold on

the UK Universal Orlando website and at brokers such as attractiontix.co.uk.

Should I buy One Park Per Day or Park to Park Tickets?
For most visitors, One Park Per Day is the best value - unless you want to ride the *Hogwarts Express*.

Ticket Pricing

Tickets are subject to seasonal pricing. These prices are for online tickets. Add $20 to these prices if you are planning on buying multi-day tickets at the park gates. Prices exclude tax.

1 Day:
Single Park (USF or IOA): Adult - $134 to $179 and Child - $129 to $144
Park to Park (USF & IOA): Adult - $189 to $234 and Child - $184 to $229

USF - Universal Studios Florida, IOA - Islands of Adventure, VB - Volcano Bay

2 Days:
One Park Per Day (USF or IOA):
Adult - $261.99 to $348.99
Child - $251.99 to $338.99

Park to Park (USF & IOA):
Adult - $321.99 to $408.99
Child - $311.99 to $398.99

Park to Park (USF & IOA & VB):
Adult - $356.99 to $443.99
Child - $346.99 to $433.99

3 Days:
One Park Per Day (USF or IOA):
Adult - $285.99 to $378.99
Child - $275.99 to $368.99

One Park Per Day (USF or IOA or VB):
Adult - $320.99 to $413.99
Child - $310.99 to $403.99

Park to Park (USF & IOA):
Adult - $345.99 to $438.99
Child - $335.99 to $428.99

Park to Park (USF & IOA & VB):
Adult - $370.99 to $473.99
Child - $360.99 to $463.99

4 Days:
One Park Per Day (USF or IOA):
Adult - $300.99 to $393.99
Child - $290.99 to $383.99

One Park Per Day (USF or IOA or VB):
Adult - $345.99 to $438.99
Child - $335.99 to $428.99

Park to Park (USF & IOA):
Adult - $365.99 to $458.99
Child - $355.99 to $448.99

Park to Park (USF & IOA & VB):
Adult - $410.99 to $500.99
Child - $400.99 to $490.99

5 Days:
One Park Per Day (USF or IOA):
Adult - $317.99 to $405.99
Child - $307.99 to $395.99

One Park Per Day (USF or IOA or VB):
Adult - $372.99 to $460.99
Child - $362.99 to $450.99

Park to Park (USF & IOA):
Adult - $387.99 to $475.99
Child - $377.99 to $465.99

Park to Park (USF & IOA & VB):
Adult - $442.99 to $530.99
Child - $432.99 to $520.99

Annual Passes

Annual passes allow you to visit the resort as often as you wish (subject to blackout dates on some passes) at a very low per-visit price. Plus, special perks are offered to Passholders, including discounts on dining and merchandise. Annual passes can be beneficial for longer visits.

	Seasonal Pass	Power Pass	Preferred Pass	Premier Pass
Price for 2-Park Pass (for guests of all ages - excludes tax)	$424.99	$474.99	$629.99	$904.99
Price for 3-Park Pass (incl. Volcano Bay)	$524.99	$584.99	$739.99	$1094.99
One Year of Unlimited Park-to-Park Admission	Blockout dates apply.	Blockout dates apply.	Yes (Blockouts apply to VB only)	Yes
Early Park Admission	No	No	Blockout dates apply.	Yes
Free self-parking (after first visit)	No	50% off	Yes	Yes
Free valet and preferred self-parking (after first visit)	No	No	No	Yes
Discounts on theme park and special event tickets	Yes	Yes	Yes	Yes
One free Halloween Horror Nights ticket (select nights only)	No	No	No	Yes
Free admission to select special events (e.g. Mardi Gras)	No	Yes	Yes	Yes
Discounted food & merchandise	No	No	Yes - 10%	Yes - 15%
Access to Universal Passholder Lounge	No	Yes	Yes	Yes
Discounts at on-site hotels	Yes	Yes	Yes	Yes
Free Universal Express Pass (after 4:00pm)	No	No	No	Yes

Blockout dates for the Power, Seasonal and Preferred Passes:
The Power and Seasonal passes theme park blockout dates (dates that you can't enter the theme parks).
• Seasonal Pass:
- January 1 and 2, 2024
- March 18 to April 6, 2024
- July 1 to 31, 2024
- November 25 to 30, 2024
- December 21 to 31, 2024

• Power Pass:
- January 1 and 2, 2024
- March 18 to 30, 2024
- December 21 to 31, 2024

Volcano Bay Blockouts:
• Preferred Pass - July 1st to August 11th 2024 before 4:00pm
• Power Pass - June 8th to August 11th 2024 before 4:00pm
• Seasonal Pass - March 18th to April 6th 2024, and June 8th to August 11th 2024

On days that a concert is performed at *Universal Studios Florida* during a non-blockout date, the *Seasonal* passes only allow access to *Universal's Islands of Adventure*. All other annual passes do allow access to the concert.

All dates in this section are inclusive.

Getting There

Before the fun begins at Universal Orlando, you need to make your way there.

....

By Car

Address: 6000 Universal Blvd, Orlando, FL.

Universal Orlando is accessible by car from Interstate 4 (I-4), where you follow Universal Blvd north to the parking area.

Parking garages open 90 minutes before the parks open. All levels except the top level are covered.

Self-parking is $30 per day, and prime parking is $50-$60. Disabled parking bays can be requested; these are closer to *CityWalk* and the theme parks. A drop-off point is also available.

After 6:00 pm, parking is free for all, except on peak dates such as *Halloween Horror Nights*.

After parking, go through *security* and walk through *CityWalk* – turn left for *Universal's Islands of Adventure* or right for *Universal Studios Florida*. For *Volcano Bay*, you board a shuttle bus from level 1. Parking is 10 minutes' walk from the theme parks.

Disney to Universal Orlando by car:
Follow Disney resort signs to Interstate 4 (I-4). Follow the I-4 North/East for 6 to 8 miles, take exit 75A, and merge onto Universal Blvd.

Shared Shuttles and Taxi Services

No public shuttle services are currently available between Orlando International Airport (MCO) and the Universal Orlando resort.

A taxi with Mears Transportation is likely to cost $80-$100 (plus tip) each way per car. UberX is priced at about $30 to $50 from Orlando International Airport to Universal depending on the size of vehicle you choose.

Public Transportation

You will be using *Lynx* - Orlando's public bus system. At the airport, board route number 42 or 111, and ask the driver for a transfer ticket - ride this bus route to the *'W Sand Lake Rd and Currency Dr'* stop (25 minutes) - this is just after Florida Mall.

Here, transfer to bus route 37 and ride this for approximately 45 minutes to the stop called *'Universal Boulevard and Hollywood Way'* which drops you off at the resort parking area.

The total journey is about 1h5-1h30m (with departures every 10-25 minutes). We recommend using *Google Maps* to guide you along. You will need exact change for the buses - the fare is $2 per person.

Disney to Universal:
Go to the Transportation and Ticket Center (TTC) or Disney Springs. Find the LYNX bus stop and catch the number 350 bus - ask the driver for a transfer ticket.

Ride the bus for about 25 minutes to the stop at *Destination Parkway and Tradeshow Boulevard*.

Here, wait for the number 38 LYNX bus and ride it until International Dr and Hollywood Way. The number 38 bus takes about 20 minutes (30 minutes at rush hour). Here you will be dropped off at Universal's parking garage where it is a 5 to 10-minute walk to the parks.

The journey time is about 55 minutes to 1 hour.

Use *Google Maps* to plan your route. You will need exact change for the buses - the fare is $2 per person.

Hotels

Deciding where to stay while on vacation can be tricky: you have to consider price, availability, size, location, and amenities to find the perfect accommodation. Luckily, central Florida is renowned for having an incredible range of options to suit all tastes and budgets.

There are numerous hotels located outside of Universal property that are cheaper than the on-site options. However, for the full Universal Orlando experience, we recommend staying at one of the on-site hotels. You will be just minutes away from the action, and the benefits of staying on-site more than justify the extra cost.

There are **four tiers** of on-site hotels:
•Value – Endless Summer Resort (Surfside Inn and Suites, and Dockside Inn and Suites)
•Prime Value – Cabana Bay Beach Resort, and Aventura Hotel
•Preferred – Sapphire Falls Resort
•Premier – Portofino Bay Hotel, Hard Rock Hotel, and Royal Pacific Resort

Benefits available to all on-site hotel guests:
•Early entry to *The Wizarding World of Harry Potter* one hour before the park opens to regular guests and to *Volcano Bay*.
•Complimentary water taxis, shuttle buses, and walking paths to both theme parks and *Universal CityWalk*.
•Complimentary delivery of merchandise purchased throughout the resort to your hotel.
•Resort-wide charging privileges. Swipe your credit card at check-in to use your room key to charge purchases to your room. At check-out, you will settle the balance as one amount.
•Optional wake-up call from a Universal character.

Guests staying at *Royal Pacific Resort, Portofino Bay Hotel*, and *Hard Rock Hotel* also enjoy these added benefits:
•FREE Universal Express Pass - Unlimited ride access to skip the regular lines in both theme parks all day.
•Priority seating at select restaurants throughout both theme parks and *CityWalk*.

All room prices in this section are nightly rates and include tax - they are based on a 3-night stay for 2 adults; food prices do not include tax.

On-Site Amenities

In this section, we cover all the essentials of staying at any of the on-site Universal Orlando hotels. From parking to pet rooms, and transportation to toning up.

Parking:
Self-parking is $28 per night ($37 for valet) at *Hard Rock Hotel, Portofino Bay,* and *Royal Pacific Resort*. The price is $26 at *Sapphire Falls*, $18 at *Cabana Bay* and *Aventura Hotel*, and $15 at the *Endless Summer resort*. Hotel guests do not get a discount on this rate.

Day guests who park in the hotel lots also pay based on the length of their stay from $10 to $45 per day.

Internet Access:
Standard in-room Wi-Fi access is complimentary. For higher speed access, there is a premium option for a daily charge.

The lobby and pool areas at all the hotels have free Wi-Fi, open to everyone including those not staying at the hotel.

Pet rooms:
Pet rooms are available at all Premier and Preferred hotels. A cleaning fee of $50 per night applies, up to a maximum of $150 per room.

Refrigerators:
All rooms include a complimentary mini-refrigerator.

Kids Camps:
Kids camps are available at *Royal Pacific Resort*, *Portofino Bay Hotel*, and *Hard Rock Hotel* in the evenings. This keeps kids occupied with activities while parents spend quality time together.

Guests from any on-site hotel can use the Kids Camps at other hotels. Details can be obtained from the concierge desk. Prices are about $15 per child per hour.

This is a group activity and not a private babysitting service, although this too can be arranged.

Smoking Rooms:
All rooms at all the on-site hotels are *non*-smoking rooms.

Early Park Admission:
All the on-site Universal hotels featured in the following pages offer complimentary early park admission to one of the two theme parks plus *Volcano Bay Water Park*.

Fitness and pools

Fitness Suites/Gyms:
All on-site hotels have complimentary gym for their guests.

Guests staying at an on-site hotel (except *Endless Summer Resort*) can use any of the fitness suites. This means that a guest from *Cabana Bay Beach Resort* could, for example, visit the gym at the *Hard Rock Hotel* with their room key.

Pools:
The on-site hotels have impressive pools and staying at most on-site resort hotels, you can use the pool of any resort (and even settle the tab at another hotel with your hotel key). A fantastic benefit! The exception to this is guests staying at *Endless Summer Resort* who cannot pool hop.

Why not try the pools at *Cabana Bay*, then splash at the *Hard Rock*, and finish the day with a dip at the *Sapphire Falls* pool?

Dining Key

Throughout this guide, you'll find plenty of information regarding dining. To provide an at-a-glance look at how much it costs to eat at a restaurant, we use the following key:

$ (Under $15) | $$ ($16 to $29) | $$$ ($30 to $39) | $$$$ ($40 to $49) | $$$$$ ($50+)

Pricing refers to a typical entree for an adult and does not reflect the cost of appetizers, desserts, drinks, tax or tip.

Endless Summer Resort

With over 2000 rooms, this Value hotel is priced for budget-conscious guests. Unlike the other hotels at Universal, this resort is not located on the main Universal resort and requires a 25-minute walk or a 5-to-10-minute complimentary shuttle bus ride.

Room Size: Standard rooms are 313 ft^2, and two-bedroom suites are 440 ft^2.
Room Prices: From $145 to $259. 2-Bedroom suites are priced from $228 to $337 per night, plus tax.
Amenities: An arcade room, fitness center, pool, and a store.

Endless Summer Resort is made up of two hotels - *Surfside Inn & Suites*, and *Dockside Inn & Suites*. The two hotels are not physically connected but guests can use facilities at both hotels - getting between them involves crossing a (major) road.

Unlike all the other Universal Orlando resorts, *Endless Summer Resort* is not connected to the main area with the two theme parks, *Volcano Bay* and *CityWalk*.

To travel from these hotels to the main area means going through public land via a main road - you can either walk this distance (approx. 1 mile) or catch the complimentary shuttle bus. The bus for the theme parks drops you off at the parking garage from where it is a 5-10 minute walk to the parks.

Standard rooms are comparable with *Aventura Hotel*, but the suites at this hotel are smaller than other suites at the Universal on-site hotels - they are priced accordingly.

There are several dining options but there is no Table Service restaurant here.

In addition to the dining options listed below, there is a Starbucks in each hotel lobby and both hotels have in-room pizza delivery.

Complimentary Express Pass access is not included for guests staying at this hotel.

Dining

Beach Break Cafe (Surfside) [$] – Serves breakfast, pizzas, salads, rotisserie options, sandwiches, burgers and other ready to go meals and beverages.
Sand Bar (Surfside) [$] – A drinks-only bar, no snacks. Drinks are $7.50-$15 each.
Pier 8 Market (Dockside) [$] – Serves breakfast, lunch and dinner in a casual style. Serves pizzas, burgers, grill items, sandwiches and soups.
Sunset Lounge (Dockside) [$] – A drinks-only bar, no snacks. Drinks are $7.50-$14 each.
The Oasis Beach Bar (Dockside) [$] – Pool bar, no snacks. Drinks are $7.50-$15 each.

Aventura Hotel

This 600-room Prime Value hotel is a big step up from Endless Summer Resort. There are walking paths to the parks and CityWalk (20-25 minutes), or you can use the free shuttle.

On-site Transportation

At the top *Preferred* and *Premier*-level hotels, your transportation options to reach the theme parks include shuttle buses, water taxis and walking paths. We do not recommend the shuttle buses as the drop-off point is a 10-minute walk from the theme parks.

Walking and water taxis are our preferred forms of transportation. Water taxis begin operating from the hotels 30 minutes before Early Park Admission. The last departure from *CityWalk* is at 2:30am year-round.

At *Cabana Bay* and *Aventura Hotel*, you can use the walking path or shuttle buses. The buses drop you off a 10-minute walk from the parks; alternatively, the walking path route takes 20 to 25 minutes.

Shuttle buses run every 10 to 15 minutes to all hotels and are even more frequent at the *Value* and *Prime Value* hotels.

Room Size: Standard rooms are 314 ft² and kids suites are 591 ft².
Room Prices: $202 to $317, for a standard room, $389 to $561 for a kids' suite.
Amenities: Arcade room; fitness center; pool and splash zone; a store; rooftop and poolside bars.

In contrast to the following resorts which have elaborate themes, this hotel aims to be the most technologically advanced place to stay at Universal.

Rooms include all the amenities you would expect and some have views over and into the theme parks.

The food hall features many different cuisines. There is no Table Service restaurant at this resort, however. There are also three bars including one on the roof offering amazing views, as well as a *Starbucks* location.

Complimentary Express Pass access, which is included in some of the more expensive on-site resorts, is *not* included here, is neither is boat access to the theme parks or *CityWalk*.

This hotel is next door to *Volcano Bay Water Park*, so you can simply walk over to this park in minutes. It is located in the main Universal theme park area.

Dining

Urban Pantry [$] – Serves breakfast options, as well as pizzas, stir fry and sushi, rotisserie food, burgers and other ready to go meals and beverages.
Bar 17 Bistro [$] – Aventura's rooftop bar on the 17th floor. Serves drinks and light bites such as cheese boards, baos, salads and burgers.
Bar Sol [$] – A drinks-only poolside bar, no food.
Bar Ventura [$] – A drinks-only lobby bar, no food

Cabana Bay Beach Resort

This 2200-room, Retro-1950s and 1960s Prime Value hotel is one of the most affordable and fun on-site options. There are walking paths to the parks and CityWalk (20 to 25 minutes) or you can use the complimentary shuttle.

Room Size: Standard rooms are 300 ft², family suites are 430 ft² and 2-bedroom suites are 772 ft²

Room Prices: $202 to $317, plus tax for a standard room. Family suites: $270 to $410. 2-bedroom suites are $488 to $748.

Amenities: A 10-lane bowling alley; arcade room; two resort pools – one with a water slide; s'mores fire pit; hot hub; poolside movies and activities; a store; and a fitness center.

Cabana Bay Beach Resort is a well-themed and fun resort in a 1950s and 1960s style. This resort is the perfect middle-ground for the location and amenities you get versus the price.

Food options include a large food court with a wide selection and food trucks outside. Plus, in-room pizza delivery. The resort's Table Service restaurant is part of the bowling alley. You are a short shuttle bus journey away from *CityWalk*, or you can walk to one of the other on-site hotels for a more upscale dinner.

Perhaps the biggest surprise is the 10-lane bowling alley, which is unheard of at any other hotel. This is $17 per adult, $12 for kids under 10, shoe rental is $4 per pair, and food is available.

There are two pools at the resort. The main pool (10,000 ft²) has a water

slide, and the 8,000 ft² pool has a sandy beach. Both pools offer accessible zero-entry ramps. The smaller pool even has a 700-foot-long lazy river around it.

Free poolside activities take place throughout the day, and there are also s'mores pits to use.

Self-service laundry is $3 per wash and $3 per dryer.

Guests staying at *Cabana Bay* do NOT receive complimentary Express Passes like at the more premium on-site hotels. However, the price difference between this hotel and those that include Express Pass access is large, so this is understandable.

There is also no water taxi service to theme parks at this hotel. However, *Cabana Bay* guests still have the option of walking paths to the two theme parks (up to 25 minutes walk), as well as continuous, complimentary shuttle bus transportation to *CityWalk*. The hotel has direct walking access to *Volcano Bay Water Park* in just a few minutes.

Dining

Atomic Tonic [$] – Poolside bar with drinks and light snacks.
Bayliner Diner [$] – Quick Service food court.
Galaxy Bowl Restaurant [$] – Table Service dining and Quick Service food.
Swizzle Lounge [$] – Bar.
Starbucks [$] – Quick Service location. Sells drinks and snacks.
The Hideaway Bar & Grill [$] – Poolside Bar & grilled fare.

Sapphire Falls Resort

This 1000-room, 83-suite resort is part of the Preferred category of on-site hotels. It features a Caribbean-inspired design.

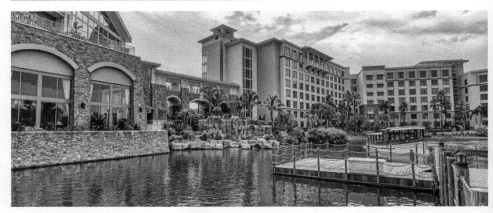

Transportation: Water taxis, walking paths (15 to 20 minutes) and shuttle buses.
Room Size: Standard rooms are 364 ft², and suites start at 529 ft².
Room Prices: $280 to $537 for a standard room. Kids suites range from $328 to $795 per night.
Amenities: A large pool, two white sand beaches, a hot tub, children's water play area with pop jets, and a water slide; fire pit for s'mores; complimentary fitness center including a dry sauna; arcade game room; and a Universal Studios Store.

This resort is a beautiful, tropical destination. It provides a step up from *Cabana Bay* in terms of amenities and theming.

The centerpiece of the resort is the 16,000ft² pool - the largest at Universal Orlando - as well as the two sandy beaches, and a waterslide. Pool-side cabanas are also available.

Standard rooms sleep up to five people – a roll-away bed is needed for the fifth person ($25 per night).

This hotel does not include Express Pass access, and guests do not receive priority seating at restaurants. Both perks are reserved for the more expensive hotels that follow.

The hotel does, however, offer complimentary water taxi services to *CityWalk* and the theme parks - usually a perk reserved for the more expensive on-site options.

Dining

Amatista Cookhouse [$$ to $$$] – Caribbean cuisine prepared in an exhibition kitchen. Whether dining indoors or out or in one of the private dining areas, feel welcomed and relaxed in this inspiring restaurant.
Drhum Club Kantine [$] – Pool bar serving a Tapas-style menu including burgers, salads and Wings, as well as drinks.
New Dutch Trading Co. [$] – With ready-to-go meals, soups, beverages, fresh-baked breads and homemade jams, this is the stop for provisions and supplies.
Strong Water Tavern [$$ to $$$]– A wall of vintage rums, a ceviche bar and a patio overlooking the lagoon make Strong Water Tavern a unique watering hole. There are also daily rum tastings, making this lounge a destination. Tapas-style dishes are served.

Royal Pacific Resort

This 1000-room, Preferred category hotel is themed to a tropical paradise.

TOP TIP

Due to the location of the dock, it is usually quicker to walk from this resort to *Islands of Adventure* and *CityWalk* than to use the water taxi service. The water taxi is, however, more relaxing.

Transportation: Water taxis, walking paths (15 to 20 minutes to the parks), and shuttle buses.
Room Size: Standard rooms are 375 ft^2, and suites start at 650 ft^2.
Room Prices: $465 to $844 for a standard room, and $785 to $1382 for a Jurassic World-themed kids suite.
Amenities: One very large pool, volleyball court, kids' water play area, fitness center, croquet, poolside activities, and the *Wantilan Luau* dinner show.

The hotel's laid-back Polynesian vibe and its location make it a solid choice - this hotel includes unlimited complimentary Express Pass access for guests.

From the moment you step inside, you are a world away from the hustle and bustle of Orlando's theme parks. Yet, they are conveniently located right next door.

There is one large pool at this hotel, a complimentary gym with a variety of cardio and free weight equipment, as well as steam and sauna facilities and a whirlpool.

An on-site coin-operated laundry is also available.

'Dive-In movies' are screened by the pool on select nights, and pool-side cabanas are available to rent from $100 per day.

The *Wantilan Luau* takes place on Saturdays at 6:00pm - tickets are $39 per child and $95 per adult in the regular section; add $20 for premium tickets.

Dining

Bula Bar and Grille [$ to $$] – Poolside bar and dining.
Islands Dining Room [$$ to $$$] – Table Service. Does not serve lunch.
Jake's American Bar [$$ to $$$] – Bar, with light snacks and larger meals.
Orchid Court Lounge and Sushi Bar [$$ to $$$$$]– Snacks, sushi, sashimi and drinks.
Wantilan Luau – Hawaiian dinner show at 6:00pm on Saturdays. Reservations are required. This is a buffet including non-alcoholic and select alcoholic drinks.

Hard Rock Hotel Orlando

This rock 'n' roll, Premier tier hotel has a mere 650 rooms, including 33 suites. It is the second most expensive hotel on-site, and the closest to the parks.

Transportation: Water taxis, walking paths (5 mins to *USF* and 10 mins to *IOA*), and shuttle buses.
Room Size: 375 ft^2 for a standard room
Room Prices: $525 to $906 per night for a standard room
Amenities: Pool, Jacuzzis, poolside movies, volleyball court, and a fitness center.

Feel like rock 'n' roll royalty at the *Hard Rock Hotel* - lively, yet laid back.

This hotel is the closest to *CityWalk* and the theme parks, and is right next door to *Universal Studios Florida*; this makes a midday dip in the pool a real possibility.

The highlight of the hotel is the huge 12,000ft^2 zero-entry, white sand pool. It even has an underwater sound system and a slide!

The hotel also has a beach with a volleyball court and lounge chairs. There are two Jacuzzis, including one for adults only.

Most nights there is a poolside 'dive-in movie,' and sometimes even dive-in concerts.

Poolside cabanas cost $80 to $250 per day, with soft drinks, bottled water, a TV, fresh fruit, towels, and a refrigerator.

You can even rent out a Fender by AXE guitar at no extra cost during your stay ($1000 refundable deposit) or a Crosley turntable with records.

Velvet Sessions – The Ultimate Cocktail Party: From January to October, on the last Thursday of each month, you can enjoy Velvet Sessions at the hotel's Velvet Bar. Each Session showcases a different type of beverage to taste, along with great live rock music.

Tickets are available in advance from velvetsessions.com or on the door and are typically $65 to $100 per person.

Dining

BeachClub [$ to $$] – Bar and Quick Service snacks.
Emack & Bolio's Marketplace [$ to $$] – Ice cream, pizzas and small bites.
The Palm Restaurant [$$$ to $$$$$] – Table Service dining, steakhouse.
The Kitchen [$$$ to $$$$] – Buffet breakfast. Table Service at lunch & dinner.
Velvet Bar [$ to $$] – Bar with light snacks and bigger plates too.

Portofino Bay Hotel

Portofino Bay is the best example of what a Premier level luxury resort should be. This 750-room hotel is incredibly well-themed to a small Italian fishing village.

The walking path is a lovely 20-minute stroll to the theme parks; take the water taxi for ultimate relaxation.

In the evenings, weather permitting, the hotel has a wonderful atmosphere with live music and classical singers.

At **Family Art Photography** you can get a family photo-shoot. Sessions last 15 to 30 minutes. Prints start at $35 each, plus tax.

Transportation: Water taxis, pedicabs, walking paths, and shuttle buses.
Room Size: 450 ft² for a standard room
Room Prices: $561 to $954 for a standard room, *Despicable Me*-themed kids suites are $1026 to $1685
Amenities: 3 pools, poolside movies, a spa, and live music.

This luxury hotel recreates the charm and romance of the seaside village of Portofino, Italy, right down to the streets and cafés.

The hotel has three pools - one with a waterslide, the other has a Jacuzzi area, and the quiet Hillside Pool overlooks the Bay.

Pool cabanas are available to rent.

The **Mandara Spa** offers a variety of indulgent experiences. A 60-minute massage starts at $190, and a 60-minute facial from $240. Nail services, waxing, and haircuts are also available. On-site guests get free fitness club access and guests who who purchase a spa or salon treatment receive a complimentary Fitness Center day pass valid on the same day.

Harbor Nights:
Four times per year, *Portofino Bay Resort* hosts 'Harbor Nights', a wine tasting and jazz event designed to capture the ambiance of the Mediterranean. Each event features select wines, gourmet food, live music, and other live entertainment.

Pricing is usually $79 per person. VIP seating is $109. All prices exclude tax. There is even a Holiday edition with a tree-lighting ceremony.

Dining

Bar American [$ to $$] – Upscale bar. Open from 5:00pm to midnight.
Bice Ristorante [$$ to $$$$] – Table Service gourmet dining.
Gelateria [$] – Serves coffees, pastries and ice creams.
Mama Della's Ristorante [$$ to $$$] – Family style Italian cuisine.
Sal's Market Deli [$ to $$] – Quick Service. Sandwiches, paninis and pizzas.
Splendido Bar & Grill [$ to $$] – Pizza, salads & sandwiches, as well as alcoholic drinks.
The Thirsty Fish Bar [$] – Bar with light snacks. Open from 6:00pm.
Trattoria del Porto [$$ to $$$] – Buffet and Table Service. Closed at lunch. The buffet breakfast is $30 per adult and $16 per child but a la carte options are also available.

Universal Studios Florida

Universal Studios Florida opened in 1990 as the Floridian cousin to the popular Universal Studios theme park in Hollywood. The original idea of the park was to experience how movies were made. Actual filming would be done in the park too.

Over the years, the park's focus has changed, and Universal now allows you to ride and "experience the movies" instead of seeing how they are made.

The park hosted 10.75 million guests in 2022.

Note: Average attraction waits noted in this section here are estimates for busy summer days during school breaks. Wait times may well be lower at other times of the year. They may also occasionally be higher, especially during the week of 4th July, Thanksgiving, Christmas, New Year, and other public holidays.

Where we list food prices, this information was accurate during our last visit to the restaurant. We include a sample of the food on offer and not the full menu. Meal prices listed do not include a drink unless otherwise stated. When an attraction is listed as requiring lockers, all loose items must be stored in complimentary locker storage outside the attraction.

Attraction Key

In the following chapters, we list each attraction individually along with some key information. Here are what the symbols in the next sections mean.

 Does it have Express Pass?

 Minimum height (in inches)

 Is there an On-Ride Photo?

 Ride/Show Length

 Average wait times (on peak days)

 Do I need to place my belongings in a locker before riding?

Production Central

Production Central is the gateway to Universal Studios Florida. You pass through it to get to the rest of the park; it contains shops and several attractions.

Production Central is home to **Guest Services** where you can request disability passes, make dining reservations, ask questions, and give feedback.

You will find lockers, **stroller and wheelchair rentals, Lost and Found**, and **First Aid**.

If you need to mail something, you can drop off your **letters and postcards** at the mailbox, located to the left as you come in after the turnstiles, to the right of the lockers.

Stamps can be purchased from the *On Location* shop.

Family & Health Services, which includes a nursing room, is here too.

TRANSFORMERS: The Ride-3D

TRANSFORMERS is a 3D screen-based moving dark ride, similar to *The Amazing Adventures of Spider-Man* at *Universal's Islands of Adventure.*

The storyline follows the *Autobots* (good guys) protecting the *AllSpark* from the *Decepticons* (bad guys). Your ride vehicle moves from set to set, acting as a moving simulator immersing you in the action.

TRANSFORMERS: The Ride is doubly impressive for fans of the franchise, though those who have not seen the movies are still likely to enjoy the action-packed experience.

A Single Rider line is available - it typically reduces your wait to about

Yes 📷 No 🔒 No | 40" ⏱ 4 mins ⏳ 30 to 60 mins

half of the regular standby line or less.

Children between 40" and 48" must be accompanied by a supervising companion.

An engineering marvel: Universal's engineers created an ingenious way to reduce the ride's footprint while keeping it long: during

the ride, while you are watching a scene on a giant screen, your vehicle goes up in an elevator up one floor that houses more of the ride. Here the ride continues and you later come back down to the first floor via another elevator while you watch another giant screen – this is all done seamlessly and really is an incredible feat.

Hollywood Rip Ride Rockit

Hollywood Rip Ride Rockit is a unique rollercoaster that dominates the skyline from the distance even before you step foot inside the park.

Once on-board, prepare to be held in by just a lap bar-style restraint as you start your vertical climb to the top for your musical thrill adventure.

🎟 Yes	📷 Yes	🔒 Yes	51-79"	⊘ 2 mins	⏳ 45 to 90 mins

You get to choose from 5 songs to play during your ride. Your choice of music will pump into your ears through individual seat speakers as your adrenaline races.

Disney fans can think of this as *Rock 'n' Roller Coaster* but without the loops and with much bigger drops.

Straight after the first drop, you enter a unique 'almost-a-loop' feature that is really fun; you do a loop but stay upright all the way around - a really unique experience.

In addition to on-ride photos, you can purchase a music video of your ride filmed using on-board cameras which includes your choice of song as the soundtrack!

A Single Rider line is available at this attraction.

Top Tip: Don't trust the Single Rider wait time that is posted at the attraction entrance - it is often exaggerated. We have often waited less than half of the official Single Rider wait time posted.

To help you estimate, in the Single Rider line, from the bottom of the stairs to being on the train is usually about 30 minutes. Feel free to ask the Team Member at the ride entrance for a better estimate.

Top Tip 2: As well as the songs on the screen, there are secret bonus songs that you can choose. To access the secret song list, after closing your restraint, push and hold the ride logo on the screen for about 10 seconds. When you let go, a number pad appears; type in a 3-digit number to load the song. A full list of the songs is available online but below we have listed a few of these. Please note you cannot purchase the on-ride video if you choose one of the secret songs.

The Secret Song List

128 – Vertigo by U2
302 – I Want You Back by The Jackson Five
306 – Lose Yourself by Eminem
308 – Run to You by Bryan Adams
309 – Save Room by John Legend
310 – Vogue by Madonna
311 – You Make Loving Fun by Fleetwood Mac

507 – Who Did You Think I Was by John Mayer Trio
703 – For Whom The Bell Tolls by Metallica
901 – Moving Right Along by The Muppets
902 – Rainbow Connection by The Muppets
904 – Night on Bald Mountain by Modest Mussorgsky

Illumination's Minion Land

The newest area of Universal Studios Florida is home to the beloved Minions from the Despicable Me franchise.

Despicable Me: Minion Mayhem

A simulator ride featuring the characters from Despicable Me. A must-do for fans of the movies!

Due to the low hourly capacity and the popularity of its characters, waits are almost always very long.

Top Tip: A stationary version of this attraction operates with benches at the front of the theater. These do not move and do not have a height requirement. When available, the wait time is usually short, e.g. 10 minutes versus 90 minutes. There is a separate queue line for this.

Yes 📷 No 🔒 No 📏 40" ✓ 4 mins ⧗ 45 to 90 mins

Children between 40" and 48" must be accompanied by a supervising companion.

Fun Fact: The trees outside the ride are banana trees as The Minions love the yellow fruit!

Illumination's Villain-Con Minion Blast

Minion Blast is the newest attraction at Universal Orlando. It is an interactive shooting ride where you use an *E-Liminator X* blaster to score points as you travel throughout *Villiancon*.

There are no ride vehicles here so you stand throughout the attraction as

 Yes 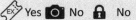 📷 No 🔒 No 📏 See below ✓ 5 mins ⧗ 15 to 30 mins

the moving walkway takes you through the scenes.

For added interactivity, download the *Universal Play* app and sync your blaster by tapping your phone to the symbol on the blaster. You

can then win virtual trophies and keep tabs on your scores when you replay.

Guests under 48" must be supervised by a companion.

Dining

Illumination's Minions Cafe [$ to $$] – Quick Service. Serves salad bowls, sandwiches, meatballs, desserts and drinks including beers.

New York

Revenge of The Mummy

Revenge of The Mummy is one of the most original and fun coasters in Orlando. It starts as a slow-moving dark ride and then turns into a traditional roller coaster themed to the world of *The Mummy*.

Although the ride does not go upside down and is not exactly the fastest attraction, it does tell its story very well and really immerses you in the atmosphere. It is a great thrill, with surprises throughout.

This unique roller coaster features fire, smoke, forward and backward motion, and more.

The queue line is also incredibly detailed and contains several interactive elements. For example, while watching guests in another location on a screen, you can press a scarab beetle and the

🎟️ Yes 📷 Yes 🔒 Yes ▮ 48" ⌄ 4 mins ⏳ 20 to 60 mins

guests will feel a quick blast of air from underneath them, guaranteed to give them a fright.

But beware where you put your hands while waiting in line, as the treasure you see around you may not be all you think it is... and you might be in for a surprise or two.

Single Riders have a dedicated queue line available. We recommend

first-timers see the regular standby line once before using the Single Rider queue.

Fun Fact: *Revenge of the Mummy* replaced *Kongfrontation* (a ride based on King Kong), that was previously housed in the same building; a statue of the great ape has been left behind as a tribute in the treasure room. See if you can spot it!

The Blues Brothers Show

See Jake and Elwood, the Blues Brothers, take to the stage in this show. Unlike other shows where you sit in a show-style amphitheater, *The Blues Brothers Show* takes place on a small stage in the street with more of a street-performer feel to it.

Crowds are not very big, and most people walk in and out during the show - it is worth stopping by this family-friendly show.

Race Through New York Starring Jimmy Fallon

This is a 3D simulated adventure with American comedian Jimmy Fallon.

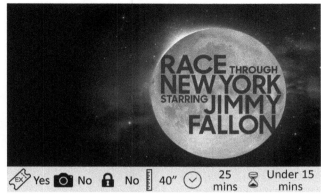

Once inside "NBC's Studios," you will be given a colored ticket and can then explore two rooms with *NBC* and *Tonight Show* memorabilia and clips from the show's 60+ year history, as well as interactive games and watch live performances. There are also seating areas. Once your color is called, you collect your 3D glasses.

Yes 🎟️ | No 📷 | No 🔒 | 40" 📏 | ✓ | 25 mins | Under 15 mins

These waiting rooms are great fun and much better than standing in a regular line. Then, board the world's first "flying theater" where Jimmy will challenge you "to a white-knuckle race."

Prepare to "speed through the streets and skies of The Big Apple, encountering everything from iconic landmarks to the deepest subway tunnels and anything else that comes to Jimmy's mind."

You will wait for about 15-20 minutes from entering the building to riding - the actual simulator ride-show is about 4 Minutes long.

Dining

Finnegan's Bar and Grill [$ to $$] – Table Service. Serves salads, sandwiches, fish and chips, chicken, corned beef, salmon and more. This is our favorite place to eat in this theme park outside of Diagon Alley.
Louie's Italian Restaurant [$ to $$] – Quick Service. Serves spaghetti and meatballs, pizza slices, whole pizza pies and fettuccine alfredo. Whole pizza pies are around $40 and jumbo slices are $20.
Starbucks and **Häagen Dasz [$]** – Quick Service, snacks and ice creams.

Springfield: Home of the Simpsons

The Simpsons Ride

The Simpsons Ride brings the famous cartoon family to life in a fun-filled simulated roller coaster ride in front of an enormous screen in *Krustyland*.

Your adventure is filled with gags throughout and is a fun family experience. Simpsons fans will love this ride!

Children between 40" and 48" must be accompanied by a supervising companion.

Fun fact: During the pre-show video, look out for the

Yes	40"	No	6 mins	No	20 to 40 mins

DeLorean car and Doc Brown from *Back to the Future*. This is a tribute to the *Back to the Future* attraction that previously occupied the same building.

Kang and Kodos' Twirl 'N' Hurl

Yes	N/A	No	1 min	No	Under 10 mins

This is a relatively standard fairground-style spinning ride, like Disney's *Dumbo* attraction.

Here, you sit in flying saucers and spin around. A lever allows you to control the height of your saucer.

Around the attraction, there are pictures of Simpsons characters; when you fly past them, they speak.

The Springfield Area: There are many photo opportunities here, including a giant Lard Lad donut sculpture, Chief Wiggum by his police car, a statue of Jebediah Springfield, Duff Man flexing his muscles and more. Characters often meet in this area, and there are carnival games you can pay to play.

Dining

Fast Food Boulevard – Quick Service. Despite looking like several separate Simpsons buildings, this is actually one area with the following sections:
- **Moe's Tavern [$]** sells Buzz Cola, Flaming Moes, and Duff Beer
- **Lisa's Teahouse of Horror [$ to $$]** sells salads and wraps
- **Luigi's [$ to $$]** sells personal-sized pizzas
- **The Frying Dutchman [$ to $$]** sells fish-based dishes
- **Cletus' Chicken Shack [$]** sells fried chicken and chicken sandwiches
- **Krusty Burger [$ to $$]** sells burgers and hot dogs

Duff Brewery [$] – Bar with snacks.
Bumblebee Man's Tacos [$] – Quick Service.

Hollywood

Universal's Horror Make Up Show

 Yes None 📷 No ⌄ 25 minutes 🔒 No ⧗ Scheduled Shows

Go behind the scenes and see how gory and horror effects are created for Hollywood movies in this fun and educational show that is sure to have you in stitches.

The script is very well thought out, with laugh after laugh, and some fun audience interaction too. This is one show we highly recommend you watch!

The theatre is relatively small, so do get there early.

If you want to be part of the show, the hosts tend to choose young women in the middle section of the theater. They also tend to go for someone who they think will speak no English, for comedic effect.

The Bourne Stuntacular

 Yes None No ⌄ 25 minutes No ⧗ Scheduled Shows

The Bourne Stuntacular is an indoor live-action stunt show based on Universal Pictures' blockbuster *Bourne* film franchise.

The show blurs the lines between the action on stage

and on the screens incredibly well.

The show is action-packed and features live performers, high-tech props and a huge LED screen that makes it impossible to tell

where the live-action ends and the cinema begins.

This is a great show, although it is not suitable for anyone who is sensitive to loud noises.

Dining

Mel's Drive In [$ to $$] – Quick Service. Serves burgers, chicken fingers and milkshakes.
Schwab's Pharmacy [$] – Snacks. Serves ice cream.
TODAY Cafe [$ to $$] – Quick Service. Serves sandwiches, pastries and salads.

San Francisco

Fast & Furious: Supercharged

Yes	40"	No	5 minutes	No	Less than 15 mins

Fast & Furious: Supercharged is a simulator-style attraction in which you take part in a simulated high-speed chase with the cast from the movies.

Fast & Furious may at times operate a Virtual Line system but most of the time you can simply walk right into the first show room. A Single Rider queue line is also available.

Fans of the franchise will likely enjoy seeing some race cars up close and some familiar faces on screen.

However, theme park fans generally agree that this is the worst ride in the park.

It is perhaps something to do when it is wet, or the waits for other rides are too long.

Children between 40" and 48" must be accompanied by a supervising companion.

Dining

Richter's Burger Co. [$] – Quick Service. Serves burgers, salads, and chicken sandwiches.
Lombard's Seafood Grille [$$ to $$$$] – Table Service. Serves salads, sandwiches, catch of the day, mussels and more.
San Francisco Pastry Company [$] – Snacks and Quick Service. Serves sandwiches, soups and pastries.

KidZone

E.T. Adventure

Yes	34"	No	5 minutes	No	Less than 20 mins

On this cute, if aging, ride you sit on bicycles, like in the *E.T.* movie, and soar through the sky while trying to keep E.T. safe.

It is a fun little ride with a relatively high capacity and one of the few *Universal Studios Florida* attractions that remains from the park's opening day.

The ride system allows you to 'cycle through the air' and makes for a truly immersive experience.

If you do not like heights, avoid this attraction.

Children between 34" and 48" must be accompanied by a supervising companion.

Animal Actors on Location!

This is a behind-the-scenes look at how animals are taught to act in films – there is even some audience participation.

Animal fans (and children) will enjoy it, but in our opinion, the show is lackluster with a significant reliance on video clips and a lack of flow.

It is a shame to see this show, especially when compared to a similar show at *Disney's Animal Kingdom Park* – Disney's show has humor, a great storyline, and a real wow factor. This one doesn't.

We would advise giving this a miss unless you are a big animal fan, have young kids to entertain or you have time to fill.

Dining

KidZone Pizza Company [$] – Quick Service. Serves pizzas, pretzels and corn dogs.

Dreamworks Land

This new area of Universal Studios Florida will open sometime in 2024. It will feature a retheme of the Woody Woodpecker Rollercoaster as well as other new attractions.

Unnamed Coaster

Yes	36"	No	44 seconds	No	Less than 30 mins

Think of this as a kid's first rollercoaster – a way to get them introduced into the world of coasters before trying something a bit more intense.

The ride is great fun for the little ones or just for those not wanting to jump on the likes of *The Incredible Hulk Coaster* just yet.

It is a short ride but should be more than enough to please young thrill-seekers.

Children between 36" and 48" must be accompanied by a supervising companion.

Other Dreamworks Land Rumors

Universal has been very light on details as to the exact elements of this new land. The official announcement states:

"Universal Orlando Resort will debut an all-new themed land featuring DreamWorks Animation's beloved animated characters.

As guests step into this new land, their imaginations will run wild as they take in the vibrant colors, sights and sounds that surround them.

They will share special moments with their favorite characters like Gabby from Gabby's Dollhouse and explore themed, interactive play spaces and attractions that bring popular franchises like Shrek, Trolls and Kung Fu Panda to life in the most imaginatively fun ways."

Rumours from OrlandoParkStop.com (which has an excellent track record) currently say that as well as the re-themed coaster mentioned above, the area will also feature a Shrek swap-themed playground area with a Shrek and Donkey meet and greet.

As far as the Trolls franchise is concerned, this could be the new theme on the rollercoaster above.

There will also be a Trolls-themed (or other Dreamworks property) theater show.

Finally, there will be a Kung Fu Panda area although we don't know if this will be a show, meet and greet or other experience.

Universal has not given an opening date for this area but we expect it to open by the end of June 2024 in time for the peak summer break.

The Wizarding World of Harry Potter: Diagon Alley

The Wizarding World of Harry Potter is one of the best-known areas at Universal, and it is split between the two theme parks. The Hogsmeade area is in Islands of Adventure, and Diagon Alley is in Universal Studios Florida.

Diagon Alley is a high street in the Harry Potter universe. As it cannot be seen by Muggles (non-Wizards), Universal has hidden this area of the park behind a recreation of London's Waterfront at *Universal Studios Florida*.

On the waterfront are façades of London landmarks. As well as Eros, there is the Knight Bus which features an interactive shrunken head experience as seen in the Prisoner of Azkaban film.

Visitors enter Diagon Alley through Leicester Square station and transition into the Wizarding World via brick walls and the help of some sound effects.

Shops

• **Quality Quidditch Supplies** – Sells apparel, hats and pendants, brooms, Snitches and Quaffles.

• **Weasleys' Wizard Wheezes** – Sells prank items, toys, novelty items and magic tricks, such as *Extendable Ears* and *Decoy Detonators*.

• **Madam Malkin's** – Find Hogwarts school uniforms, with ties, robes, scarves, and more. Also sells jewelry themed to the four school houses.

• **Ollivanders** (show and shop) – See a short show in which a wand picks a wizard. Then, you can opt to buy your own wand.

• **Wiseacre's Wizarding Equipment** – Stocks a wide range of items from hourglasses to compasses, and telescopes to binoculars.

• **Wands by Gregorovitch** – The legendary wand shop.

• **Shutterbuttons** – Get a personalized "moving picture" just like the Harry Potter newspapers for $89.95. Up to 4 people can take part in the experience. You are supplied with robes, but you must bring your own wand.

Ollivanders

 No None No 3 minutes No Less than 10 minutes

Technically, this is a pre-show to a shop. You enter *Ollivanders* in groups of 25 people.

Next, one person is chosen by the wand-master to find the right wand for them through a short, interactive show with special effects. When the right wand is found, they are given the option to buy it as everyone exits to the shop next door.

This is a fantastic experience that we highly recommend you visit. It is suitable for all ages.

The queue line at this *Ollivanders* moves much more quickly than the one in *Islands of Adventure*.

Dining

Fans of the boy wizard will not go hungry in *Diagon Alley*:
•**Leaky Cauldron [$ to $$]** – Quick Service. Serves English fare such as Bangers and Mash, Toad in the Hole, Fish and Chips and more.

•**Florean Fortescue's Ice Cream [$]** – Quick Service. Serves ice cream and other treats, as well as breakfast items and pastries in the morning.

Ice Cream flavors include

Earl Grey and Lavender, Clotted Cream, Orange Marmalade, Butterbeer, and others. We highly recommend the Butterbeer ice cream – there is even an option with a souvenir glass.

Knockturn Alley

Running alongside Diagon Alley is the darker *Knockturn Alley*, described as a "gloomy back street" by Universal. The shops and storefronts here are filled with items related to Dark Magic.

The flagship store here is *Borgin and Burkes*, which sells dark items such as Death Eater masks, skulls, and other sinister objects. Make sure to check out the vanishing cabinet.

This area is covered, so it is always dark and creates a nighttime atmosphere. It is popular during Orlando's frequent rain showers.

Be sure to look out for the animated "Wanted" posters

of the Death Eaters.

Check out the window with the tarantulas on it - though it may give you more than you bargained for if you get too close.

There are also many

interactive wand experiences available in this area (more on these later).

Two other streets in *Diagon Alley* have themed shopfronts and interactive wand touches – *Horizont Alley* and *Carkitt Market*.

Early Entry to the Wizarding World

Staying on-site at a Universal hotel entitles you to early admission into the *WWOHP* one hour before the general public.

This also applies to off-site hotels booked as part of a Universal vacation package online or through an

authorized reseller – check this is included in your booking.

Either *Diagon Alley* or *Hogsmeade* will be open. This changes regularly; check Universal's website to find out which one.

If you do not have early admission, be at the park entrance in advance; guests are often allowed into the park up to 30 minutes before the officially published opening time.

Learn more about Early Park Admission on page 67.

Attractions

Harry Potter and the Escape from Gringotts

Outside Gringotts Bank, marvel at the fire-breathing dragon on the roof. Then, head inside and prepare for the experience of a lifetime.

Just like *Harry Potter and the Forbidden Journey* in *Islands of Adventure*, the queue line is as much of an experience as the ride itself. The storyline begins to unfold as you see signs of Harry, Ron, and Hermione discussing their plans.

EXP Yes | 42" | Yes | 5 mins | Yes | 30 to 60 mins

The ride itself is a "multidimensional" rollercoaster-type attraction. It mixes real-world sets with 3D video on huge screens.

There are drops and turns in the layout (but the ride never goes upside down), and it is more a 3D-style ride than a rollercoaster - more like *TRANSFORMERS* than *The Incredible Hulk*. The ride features 4K-high definition technology as well as 3D screens, with glasses worn by riders.

Apart from one drop and a short high-speed section, this is not a hugely thrilling coaster. You are there for the story and not huge thrills.

Single Riders have a dedicated queue line, but it skips all the queue line scenes and leads directly to the loading area. The Single Rider line *can* save you a considerable amount of time.

Children between 32" and 48" must be accompanied by a supervising companion.

Storyline – Spoiler Alert: The ride is inspired by the final movie, *Harry Potter and the Deathly Hallows – Part 2*. In this instalment, Harry, Ron, and Hermione break into Gringotts bank to steal a powerful Horcrux to help them defeat Lord Voldemort. On *Harry Potter and the Escape from Gringotts*, you encounter the trio during this quest – but expect to meet some dangerous creatures and malicious villains as well!

During the ride, you will come face-to-face with Bellatrix Lestrange, security trolls, fire-breathing dragons, and even Voldemort himself.

Interactive Wand Experiences

Interactive wand experiences are available at *The Wizarding World*, both at *Diagon Alley* and *Hogsmeade*.

To participate, guests must purchase an interactive wand from the *Wizarding World*'s shops. These are $63; this is $8 more than the non-interactive wands.

Once you have purchased a wand, look for one of the 25+ bronze medallions embedded in *The Wizarding World*'s streets that mark locations you can cast spells. You also get a map of the sites included with each wand purchase.

Once standing on a medallion, perform the correct spell: draw the shape of the spell in the air with your wand and say the spell's name. Then, watch the magic happen.

This is a fun bit of extra entertainment, and wands can be reused on future visits.

Kings Cross Station and the Hogwarts Express

At *Kings Cross Station*, break through the wall onto Platform 9 ¾, and catch the *Hogwarts Express*. This real train ride transports you to *Hogsmeade Station* (at *Universal's Islands of Adventure*) - the other Universal theme park.

Yes	N/A	No	15-45 mins	No	15 to 45 mins

On the 5-minute journey, as you look out of the train windows, you will see stories unfold – all on a full-sized train just like in the movies.

During the journey, you may see Hagrid on his motorcycle, the English countryside, Buckbeak the Hippogriff, the purple Knightbus, the Weasley twins, and even some Dementors. There are many more surprises in store, of course, and not everything happens *outside* the train carriage.

Each of the *Hogwarts Express* trains seat 200 passengers, and the story is unique in each direction.

Once you hop off the train at *Hogsmeade*, you can explore the area and its attractions, including the incredible *Harry Potter and the Forbidden Journey* ride.

Important: To experience the *Hogwarts Express*, you must have a *Park-to-Park* ticket as you will physically move between two theme parks. *A Single-Park* ticket does not allow you to experience this ride – guests with Single Park tickets can experience each of the theme parks' Wizarding Worlds on separate days, but cannot travel on the *Hogwarts Express*.

Diagon Alley Live Entertainment

At *Carkitt Market*, two shows are performed daily:

The first brings to life two fables from "The Tales of Beedle the Bard" – *The Fountain of Fair Fortune* and *The Tale of the Three Brothers*. This trunk show uses set pieces, props, and puppetry.

The second soul-filled show features a musical performance by *The Singing Sorceress: Celestina Warbeck and the Banshees*.

As well as the live stage shows, the area hosts other interactive experiences. Just outside Diagon Alley, you will find the *Knight Bus* and its two occupants: a shrunken head and the Knight Bus Conductor. Both are happy to chat, joke around, and take photos.

At *Gringotts Money Exchange,* you can swap Muggle currency (US$) for Wizarding Bank Notes, which can be used at both Universal parks to purchase snacks and in stores.

Stores in *The Wizarding World*, of course, accept regular US dollars and credit or debit cards, but these Potter banknotes are a cool souvenir.

World Expo

MEN IN BLACK: Alien Attack

| 🎟️ Yes | 📏 42" | 📷 Yes | ✓ 5 minutes | 🔒 Yes | ⏳ Less than 45 mins |

At *Men In Black*, your mission is to protect the city and defeat the attacking aliens.

You are sent in teams of six in vehicles and, using hand-held laser blasters, compete against another group of riders to defeat the aliens and get a high score.

This ride is a fun, family-friendly experience that we highly recommend. A Single Rider line is available.

Children between 42" and 48" must be accompanied by a supervising companion.

Top Tip: Hold down the trigger throughout the ride.

You get points for doing this, regardless of whether you hit any targets or not.

Top Tip 2: For major points, shoot Frank the Pug who is hidden on the ride in the newspaper stand on the right side of the second room.

Universal's Islands of Adventure

....

Universal's Islands of Adventure opened in 1999 with many famed attractions such as *The Incredible Hulk Coaster* and *The Amazing Adventures of Spider-Man*, which instantly put it on the world theme park map.

The true revolution for the park, however, came with the opening of *The Wizarding World of Harry Potter: Hogsmeade* in 2010.

Expansion and innovation in the park have not stopped since the *Wizarding World* was unveiled. In this theme park, you will not find 'lands' or areas, but 'islands' instead. Together these islands make up *Universal's Islands of Adventure*.

The park hosted 11 million guests in 2022.

Live Entertainment at the Park:
There are no daily fireworks shows or parades at this park.

There are, however, character appearances throughout the various lands, in particular in *Seuss Landing* and *Marvel Superhero Island*. There are no Harry Potter characters in *Hogsmeade*, except for the Hogwarts Express Conductor.

Port of Entry

Perhaps the most beautiful entrance to a theme park in Orlando, Port of Entry transports you to a different time and place.

There are no attractions in this area of the park. Instead, *Port of Entry* acts as an entranceway to the *Islands of Adventure* themselves.

You will find many shops and a few places to eat in this area.

To the right of the welcome arch at *Port of Entry*, you will find **Guest Services**. Here, you can get help with accessibility, dining reservations, as well as questions, positive feedback, and complaints. **Lost and Found** is also located here.

Lockers are located to the left of the archway.

Strollers and **wheelchair rentals** can also be found here. **First Aid** is located inside the *Open Arms Hotel* building to the right of the entrance archway. There is another First Aid station in *The Lost Continent* by the bazaar.

Fun fact: At the wheelchair and stroller rental location, look out for a sign listing the prices of rentals along with several gag items, which have already been "rented out" including a gondola, an aero boat, and a rocket car.

Dining

Confisco Grille and Backwater Bar [$ to $$] – Table Service. Serves soups, salads, curries and thai dishes, sandwiches and pasta. Backwater Bar is a full-service bar.
Croissant Moon Bakery [$] – Quick Service. Serves continental breakfasts, sandwiches, paninis, cakes, and branded coffee.
Starbucks [$] – Quick Service.

Seuss Landing

This area is themed to the Dr. Seuss books. To make this land look unique, the theme park designers even made sure there were no straight lines anywhere

One Fish, Two Fish, Red Fish, Blue Fish

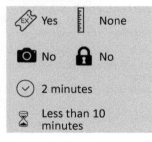 Yes 📷 No 🔒 No | See below | ⌄ 90 secs | ⧖ 15 to 45 mins

A classic spinning ride, like *Dumbo* in the Disney parks. This one, however, packs a bit of a twist.

The soundtrack is actually a set of instructions you should follow to stay dry. So when you hear "up, up, up" you will want to steer

yourself upwards and be as high as possible to avoid a soaking. This is a fun twist on what can be a bit of an unimaginative type of ride. At colder times the water is turned off.

Children under 48" (1.22m) must ride with an adult.

The High in the Sky Seuss Trolley Train Ride

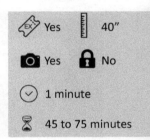

🎟 Yes   📏 40"

📷 Yes   🔒 No

⌄ 1 minute

⧖ 45 to 75 minutes

This cute, slow train journey ventures across the rooftops of *Seuss Landing*.

The minimum height is 40" (1.02m) to rid accompanied, or 48" (1.22m) to ride alone.

Caro-Seuss-el

🎟 Yes   📏 None

📷 No   🔒 No

⌄ 2 minutes

⧖ Less than 10 minutes

This classic carousel-type ride is themed to the Seuss books.

There is usually no wait for this ride.

The Cat in the Hat

🎟 Yes   📏 36"

📷 No   🔒 No

⌄ 4 minutes

⧖ 15 to 45 minutes

Spin through the story of *The Cat in the Hat*. The ride makes more sense if you have read the books or seen the movies, but it is enjoyable for everyone.

The Lost Continent

Themed to mythological creatures; home to acclaimed restaurant, Mythos.

The Mystic Fountain

A witty, talking, interactive fountain in a courtyard area. You can ask the fountain questions and have a chat.

The fountain also loves to tell jokes and to get people wet if they come too close! The fountain only operates at select times of the day.

Dining

Mythos Restaurant [$ to $$] – Table Service. Serves sandwiches, pad thai, salmon, and pasta dishes. This is our favorite in-park restaurant.
Fire Eater's Grill [$ to $$] – Quick Service. Serves gyros, cheese dogs, chicken fingers, and salads. Large portions.
Doc Sugrue's Desert Kebab House - Quick Service. Serves kebabs and Greek salads.

Fun Fact: Stand under the bridge behind *Mythos Restaurant* to hear a troll.

Skull Island

Skull Island: Reign of Kong

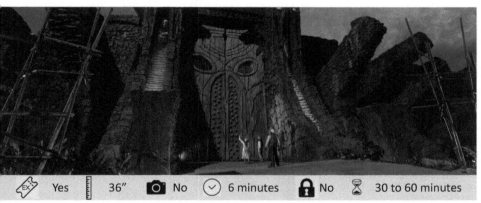

EXP	Yes		36"	📷	No	✓ 6 minutes	🔒 No	⏳ 30 to 60 minutes

Step aboard one of the huge 72-seat 4x4 vehicles. Once onboard, each ride promises to be unique as one of five different drivers takes you on an adventure.

Universal puts it best: "You'll navigate perilous jungles, explore ancient temple structures, and encounter hostile natives – and that's only the beginning."

"Throughout the rest of your excursion, you'll brave foreboding caves crawling with prehistoric creatures, fend off unspeakable terrors – and even come face-to-face with the colossal Kong himself."

The animatronics, music, and atmosphere created here are second to none.

This ride features a Single Rider line - wait times here are usually about half of the regular queue line.

Top Tip: Although each side provides a different and unique experience, if you want to see King Kong up close, sit on the right side of the vehicle. The drivers also change up the experience too.

Warning: The queue line for this ride is dark and may scare young children. The ride may also be too intense for them.

The Wizarding World of Harry Potter: Hogsmeade

Harry Potter and the Forbidden Journey

This truly ground-breaking ride features projections, sets, and floating ride vehicles. The queue line is an attraction unto itself, as you wind your way through Hogwarts castle watching scenes and experiencing moments like the famous trio in the Potter universe.

At the end of the queue, it is time for an incredible adventure - this is a simulator-style attraction that blurs the lines between physical sets and on-screen projections. Plus, the moment your enchanted bench first takes off is breathtaking.

Expect to encounter Dementors, take part in a quidditch match, come face to face with dragons, and much more.

EX✓ Yes   48"   📷 Yes   ⊘ 5 mins   🔒 Yes   ⏳ 30 to 60 mins

There is a Single Rider queue line available, which can cut down wait times significantly; waits are usually about 50-75% shorter than the standard wait time in our experience, but this will vary.

Warning: We feel this ride creates mental strain due to the simulated sensations and the screens in front of you. This means that if you ride it more than once back-to-back, you are likely to feel unwell.

Hidden Secret: When you are in Dumbledore's office hearing his speech, look at the books on the wall to the right of him. One of the books may do something very magical.

Flight of the Hippogriff

On this small rollercoaster, you soar on a Hippogriff past Hagrid's hut. Good family fun and a good starter coaster before putting your children on the likes of *The Hulk*.

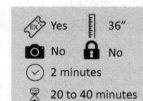

EX✓ Yes   36"

📷 No   🔒 No

⊘ 2 minutes

⏳ 20 to 40 minutes

Hogsmeade Entertainment

Triwizard Spirit Rally - A 6-minute dance contest between two wizard schools: men versus women. The men's routine involves complex sword-fighting techniques, while the ladies dazzle with their ribbons and acrobatics. It is fun, and a great photo opportunity.

Frog Choir - 9 minutes of songs performed by Hogwarts students and their frogs, all done a capella with no instruments. There is a beatbox flair to this show.

Ollivanders - Like *Ollivanders* at *Diagon Alley* but wait times are longer here. Not listed on the park map and there is no wait time sign. Enter to the left of the *Ollivanders* shop.

Hogsmeade Station and the Hogwarts Express

Catch the *Hogwarts Express*, and be transported through the countryside to *Kings Cross Station* (at *Universal Studios Florida*).
As you look out of the windows, you will see stories unfold.

Yes	N/A	No	5 mins	No	15 to 45 mins

Once you hop off the train at *Kings Cross,* you will be by the London waterfront. There, you can enter Diagon Alley for its attractions, including *Harry Potter and*

the Escape from Gringotts.

Important: Guests must have a Park-to-Park ticket to ride. Single Park tickets do not allow entry.

Hagrid's Magical Creatures Motorbike Adventure

This family-friendly roller coaster launches you at speeds of up to 50 mph as you encounter magical creatures in the Forbidden Forest. You will go forwards, backward, and drop as you ride on a motorbike.

You have the option of either sitting on the bike itself or the sidecar. This ride is a great fun and thrilling addition to the park and a must-do.

Single Riders have a dedicated line available.

No	48"	Yes	3 mins	Yes	90 to 150 mins

Shops

At *The Wizarding World*, the shops are as much of the experience as the rides.
•**Filch's Emporium of Confiscated Goods** – The exit shop of *Forbidden Journey*. Sells apparel, mugs, photo frames, dark magic items, and trinkets.
• **Honeydukes** – Those with a sweet tooth will find love potion sweets, chocolate frogs (with collectible trading cards), and more.
•**The Owlery and Dervish & Banges** – Sells wands,

Horcrux replicas, clothing, stationery, and even a model of the Hogwarts Express.
•**The Owl Post** – A real post office where you can send letters or postcards with a Hogsmeade postmark and stamp. Also sells stationery.

Restaurants

The restaurants in Hogsmeade are well-themed, and the Quick Service food is some of the best in the park. We recommend you take a look inside these, even if you do not eat there.

• **Hog's Head [$]** – Quick Service. This pub is located in the same building as *Three Broomsticks*. Serves alcoholic beer, non-alcoholic Butterbeer, and juices.
• **Three Broomsticks [$ to $$]** – Quick Service. Serves

breakfast meals. At lunch and dinner, you will find Cornish pasties, fish & chips, shepherd's pie, smoked turkey legs, rotisserie chicken, and spareribs. Family platters for 4 people are available for $73.

Jurassic Park

Jurassic Park River Adventure

On a boat, glide past enormous dinosaurs. However, this calm river adventure soon changes course. Watch out for the T-Rex before your 85-foot drop! A Single Rider line is available at this at t raction.

Top Tip: The back row typically gets you less wet.

Note: Lockers are optional and cost $4 for 90 minutes.

Yes	42"	📷 Yes	⊘ 5 mins	🔒 No	⧗ 45 to 90 mins

Camp Jurassic

This play area is themed to the Jurassic Park movies. We definitely recommend exploring the area, as the detail is just incredible.

This play area isn't only for kids. Anyone can explore it, from the caves to the water jets and the treetop plat f orms to the slides.

Fun Fact: Step on the dinosaur footprints for a roaring sound.

Jurassic Park Discovery Center

An exploration area where you can see model dinosaurs, play dinosaur-themed carnival-style games, learn about DNA sequencing, and witness a dinosaur birth.

Pteranodon Flyers

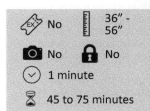

No	36" - 56"
📷 No	🔒 No
⊘ 1 minute	
⧗ 45 to 75 minutes	

Soar above Jurassic Park on a winged dinosaur glider. Guests over 56" must be accompanied by someone *under* 36" tall to ride.

Jurassic World VelociCoaster

This is park's latest and newest extreme coaster - it opened in 2021. Here you enter the paddocks where the velociraptors live and must escape.

This intense ride features 2 launches, one of which

Yes	📷 Yes	🔒 No	51"	⊘ 90 secs	⧗ 90 to 120 mins

speeds you up to 70 mph in 2.4 seconds, there are 12 seconds of air time (the 'out of your seat' feeling), an360-degree roll over the *Islands of Adventure* lagoon

and at the highest point you'll be 155 feet high.

This is the most thrilling ride at the resort and perfect for adrenaline junkies!

Dining

The Burger Digs [$ to $$] – Quick Service. Serves burgers, grilled chicken and chicken sandwiches.
Thunder Falls Terrace [$ to $$] – Quick Service. Serves cheeseburgers, ribs, salads and rotisserie chicken. The portions are large.

Toon Lagoon

Toon Lagoon is an entire land dedicated to water, with two of the park's major water attractions here - expect to get wet.

Dudley Do-Right's Ripsaw Falls

🎟️ Yes	📏 44"	📷 Yes	✓ 7 minutes	🔒 No	⏳ 45 to 75 minutes

Want a water ride that gets you absolutely soaked? Give this one a try.

The ride contains a well-themed interior and features several drops with a final rollercoaster-style splashdown making sure you leave thoroughly drenched. The ride reaches a top speed of 45mph (over 70 km/h), so you're also in for a thrill!

This ride features a Single Rider queue line.

Optional lockers are available for a fee of $4 for 90 minutes.

Popeye & Bluto's Bilge-Rat Barges

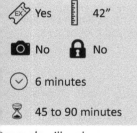

🎟️ Yes   📏 42"

📷 No   🔒 No

✓ 6 minutes

⏳ 45 to 90 minutes

Popeye's will make sure you come out drenched from head to toe. This is by far the wettest water ride at Universal, and it is a whole lot of fun! Universal has come up with creative ways to get you drenched.

Optional lockers are available costing $4 for 90 minutes; the center of the raft has a covered section for basic water protection too.

Me Ship, The Olive

This is a kids' play area and a great place for a break from the crowds.

For the pranksters among you who like causing chaos, there are free water cannons on the top level of the ship to spray guests on the *Popeye* ride below.

Dining

Blondie's [$ to $$] – Quick Service. Serves sandwiches, made to order subs and hot dogs.
Comic Strip Cafe [$ to $$] – Quick Service. Serves ramen, pizzas, salads and sandwiches.
Wimpy's Burgers [$ to $$] – Quick Service. Serves burgers and chicken fingers.

Marvel Super Hero Island

*This island contains two of our favorite attractions in all of Universal Orlando –
Spider-Man and The Incredible Hulk. There is also fun comic book theming, places
to eat and shop, and other attractions. You will often find Marvel characters
meeting guests in this area of the park.*

The Amazing Adventures of Spider-Man

🎟️ Yes	📏 40"	📷 Yes	⏱️ 5 minute	🔒 No	⏳ 45 to 75 minutes

One of the most ground-breaking rides in the world, *The Amazing Adventures of Spider-Man* is a world-class attraction that incorporates projection screens with real-world elements like never seen before.

More than 20 years after opening, the attraction has not aged a single bit, as it has been updated with 4K and 3D technology, creating higher resolution images. The storyline works as well as it ever has.

The ride is a fun experience swinging around New York City with Spider-Man. It is an absolute must-do.

This ride operates a Single Rider line, which can often save you a lot of time.

Doctor Doom's Fearfall

🎟️ Yes	📏 52"	📷 No	⏱️ 45 seconds	🔒 No	⏳ 45 to 60 minutes

Love drop towers? Then you will adore this ride.

Doctor Doom needs your screams for power; to get them, he shoots you up in the air – and he will definitely get more than enough power.

The ride consists of one high-speed launch up, followed by a free-fall back down (and then up and down until you stop).

This attraction operates a Single Rider queue line – ask for it at the entrance.

Fun Fact: Look at the ground outside the attraction for chalk outlines of the Fantastic Four. They, too, went on the ride and came plummeting to the ground, landing where the outlines are. A subtle detail, but really cool once you notice it.

The Incredible Hulk Coaster

| EX | Yes | 54" | 📷 Yes | ⌄ 2 minutes | 🔒 Yes | ⏳ 30 to 90 minutes |

Winner of numerous awards, *The Incredible Hulk Coaster* is our favorite roller coaster in all of Orlando.

It is a truly outstanding thrill with huge loops, an underground section, and non-stop fun from the moment you are launched out of the tunnel until you are back at the station.

There is a Single Rider line at this attraction; just ask the ride attendant at the front to use it – the waits for it are often short as it is not well signposted.

Storm Force Accelatron

| EX | Yes | 48" | 📷 No | ⌄ 1 minute | 🔒 No | ⏳ Less than 10 minutes |

This is a standard spinning teacup-style ride themed to Marvel superhero, Storm - and it's fast! An adult must accompany those under 48 inches (1.22m) tall.

Dining

Captain America Diner [$ to $$] – Quick Service. Serves burgers, chicken sandwiches, chicken fingers, and salads.
Cafe 4 [$ to $$] – Quick Service. Serves pizza, pasta, sandwiches, and salads. Whole pizza pies are $35 to $40. A Marvel Character Dinner runs here Thursday to Sunday from 5:00 pm to 7:00pm and is priced at $53 per adult and $30 per child.

Volcano Bay

Volcano Bay is Universal Orlando's water park based around an enormous, 200-foot-tall volcano - Krakatau.

Transport

Universal Orlando is in a unique situation where it is landlocked on all four sides and therefore has to be creative about its use of land. As such, *Volcano Bay* is located on a small parcel of land next to *Cabana Bay Beach Resort*.

Volcano Bay does not have a parking lot; guests staying off-site will need to park at the same Universal parking garages used for the theme parks and catch a complimentary shuttle bus to *Volcano Bay*.

Guests of all on-site hotels (except *Cabana Bay* and *Aventura Hotel*) also have a complimentary shuttle bus from the hotel to the water park. Guests staying at *Cabana Bay* and *Aventura Hotel* can walk to *Volcano Bay* as it is right next door.

TapuTapu

Universal has attempted to revolutionize the concept of a water park by creating a park free from queue lines.

To do this, you will need a waterproof wearable band called a *TapuTapu* - it is similar to a Magicband at Disney, but with a screen. It is given to you for use during the day once you are inside *Volcano Bay* - you must return it when leaving the park.

The *TapuTapu* allows you to

do several things:
• **TapTu Ride** - The attractions at *Volcano Bay* do not have standard queue lines. Instead, outside each attraction, you will see a totem pole and a posted wait time. Tap your *TapuTapu* on the totem pole to get a return time. Then, simply return to the ride entrance when your wristband vibrates to alert you. You will have to wait in a short queue to enter (usually 5-10 minutes, though at peak periods it

could be up to 30 minutes). You can only virtually queue for one attraction at a time.
• **TapTu Play** - Throughout the park, you will find interactive elements - at these, tap your *TapuTapu* and special events will be triggered, such as a spray of water onto the lazy river or lights inside a cave.
• **TapTu Pay** - Using the Universal Orlando app, you can link your park tickets and *TapuTapu* to a payment card and then use your wearable to pay throughout

the day. You can also set spending limits and add a PIN when paying.
• **TapTu Snap** - Throughout the park there are framed photo spots, simply tap your *TapuTapu* and pose. On-ride photos can also be obtained using your wristband. All these photos will appear on the Universal Orlando app, and you can buy full-quality versions there.
• **TapTu Lock** - Use your *TapuTapu* to unlock your park locker (extra charge) - you can assign up to 4 wristbands to one locker using the locker screen.

Lockers

There are four-in park locations to rent lockers at *Volcano Bay*: near Kohola Reef Restaurant, near Bambu, near Whakawaiwai Eats, and next to Waturi Marketplace. Lockers come in three sizes from small to large, priced at $10, $16, and $20 for the day.

You can store and retrieve items from the lockers as many times as you would like throughout the day. You can pay with card, cash, your room key, or your *TapuTapu* linked to a payment card. In all cases, you will need a *TapuTapu* to access your locker.

Cabana and premium seating (see below) include the use of a complimentary locker.

There are also lockers just outside *Volcano Bay*'s entrance. These are operated using a credit card and are not anywhere near as convenient as the in-park lockers.

We would only recommend using the lockers outside the park if there are no in-park lockers left.

Cabana Rentals and Premium Seating

To truly maximize your *Volcano Bay* experience, why not take advantage of one of the premium upgrade options?

• **Premium Seating** - If you want to avoid having to search for a sun lounger, this is the perfect option. Premium Seating is a set of 2 sun loungers with a sun-blocking shade, a locker, and a shared server who takes food and drink orders. Pricing is $30 to $150 per day, depending on the season.
• **Cabana Rentals** - The ultimate in luxury, there are several different varieties of cabanas for you to choose from. All include sun loungers, a fridge with bottled water, complimentary fruit, a cabana attendant and towels. The top feature is a tablet that allows you to reserve your place in line for any of the park's rides from your cabana without having to tap your *TapuTapu* physically. A single cabana for up to 6 people is $160 to $450 on the lower level and $200 to $700 on the raised level. A family suite for up to 16 people is $350 to $900.

Attractions

For each attraction, we list minimum height requirements and maximum guests' weight restrictions.

Krakatau:
At the heart of the park, you'll see the 200-foot-tall volcano called *Krakatau*. By day, you'll see its majestic waterfalls. And by night, the volcano illuminates with blazing lava.

Three body slides are at the rear of the volcano; each starts with trap doors that drop from beneath you:
• *Ko'okiri Body Plunge*: (48", 300 lbs) A racing, 70-degree drop that plummets 125-feet through the center of *Krakatau*. It is the world's first slide to travel through a pool filled with guests.
• *Kala and Ta Nui Serpentine Body Slides*: (48", 275 lbs) Two intertwining drop slides

where you'll fall freely along 124 twisting feet. Green is more intense than blue.
• *Punga Racers*: (42", 49" to ride alone, 150 lbs) A high-speed race through four different enclosed slides on manta-shaped mats.
• *Krakatau Aqua Coaster*: (42", 49" to ride alone, 700 lbs combined) The park's star attraction where you sit in canoes and travel up and down through the park's iconic volcano on a 4-person water rollercoaster.

Wave Village:
Located at the base of *Krakatau*, Wave Village is a perfect place to soak in the sun and relax on the sandy shores. It includes:
• *Waturi Beach*: (Under 48" must wear a life vest) A wave pool where you can swim, relax on the sand or indulge in private, one- or two-story cabanas.
• *The Reef*: (Under 48" must wear a life vest) An adjacent leisure pool with calmer waters and views of riders on the Ko'okiri Body Plunge.

River Village:
River Village offers several family-friendly attractions and experiences.
• *Kopiko Wai Winding River*: (Under 48" must wear a life vest) A gentle, winding river that passes through the volcano's hidden caves, featuring spontaneous water effects and a journey through the cave of starlight.
• *Tot Tiki Reef*: (Max 48") A toddler play area with spraying Maori fountains, slides, and a kid-size volcano.
• *Runamukka Reef*: (Max 54") A three-story water playground inspired by the coral reef with twisting slides, sprinklers, and more.
• *Honu*: (48", 700 lbs combined) An adventurous, 2 to 5-passenger raft ride that soars across a dual wall.
• *Ika Moana*: (42", 49" to ride alone, 750 lbs combined) A twisting, 2 to 5-passenger raft ride across bubbling geysers.

Rainforest Village:
Features an incredible assortment of attractions for thrill-seekers, including:
• *Maku*: (42", 49" to ride alone, 1050 lbs combined) A "saucer ride" sending 2 to 6- person rafts around three saucer-shaped curves.
• *Puihi*: (42", 49" to ride alone, 850 lbs combined) A 3 to 6-passenger raft ride that plunges you into darkness before bursting into a funnel and a zero-gravity drop.
• *Ohyah and Ohno Drop Slides*: (48") Two twisting, adrenaline-pumping slides that launch you 4- or 6-feet above the water at the end. You must be able to swim as the end pool is 10ft deep.
• *TeAwa The Fearless River*: (42" with a life vest, 49" to ride alone without life vest) An action-packed, racing torrent river where you ride in your inner tube amidst roaring, whitewater rapids.
• *Taniwha Tubes*: (42", 49" to ride alone, 300 lbs single or 450 lbs combined) Four unique Easter Island-inspired slides with rafts for single or double riders.
• *Puka Uli Lagoon*: (Under 48" must wear life vest) A tranquil pool; relax.

Express Pass:
Guests with an Express Pass can ride without needing to reserve a time with their *TapuTapu*. They must, however, wait in the queue once they enter each queue. Hotels do *not* include complimentary Express Pass access to *Volcano Bay;* this add-on must be purchased separately and it may sell out in advance. A 'Universal Express Pass' which offers one-time express access to 8 selected rides, is $20-$80 per day, where a 'Universal Express Plus' offers one-time express access to 12 ride for $50-$120.

Dining

Whakawaiwai Eats [$ to $$] – Quick Service. Serves pizza, salads, hot dogs, and mac & cheese.
The Feasting Frog [$ to $$] – Quick Service. Serves tacos and nachos.
Bambu [$ to $$] – Quick Service. Serves burgers, salads, and sandwiches.
Dancing Dragon's Boat Bar [$ to $$] – Bar with drinks and snacks.
Kanuku Boat Bar [$ to $$] – Bar with drinks and snacks.
Kohola Reef Restaurant & Social Club [$ to $$] – Quick Service. Serves fried chicken, burgers, pizzas, seafood, ribs and salads.

CityWalk

CityWalk is located just outside the theme parks and within walking distance of all the on-site hotels. There are shops, restaurants, bars, a movie theater and clubs.

CityWalk is Universal Orlando's entertainment district, open from 11:00 am to 2:00 am daily - admission is free.

CityWalk is often compared to *Disney Springs*, but this location is much smaller and *CityWalk* also has more of an adult feel to it, particularly at nighttime, when there is a focus on the club-like atmosphere. The shops and dining locations are also much more limited. It still, however, manages to keep a fun and friendly atmosphere no matter the time of day.

Parking is charged before 6:00 pm at the main Universal parking garages for the theme parks. After 6:00 pm, parking is free.

For restaurant and attraction hours, recorded

information is available on (407) 363-8000.

CityWalk has its own Guest Services outpost, which is well signposted and is by the restrooms. Also located nearby is **First Aid**.

Dining

CityWalk is filled with unique dining experiences. Prices quoted for entrées are for adult meals; kids meals are much cheaper.

Quick Service:

Auntie Anne's Pretzel Rolls [$] – Serves soft pretzels and hot dogs.

Bend the Bao [$] – Serves baos, sake and beers.

Bread Box Handcrafted Sandwiches [$ to $$] – Serves sandwiches and salads.

Burger King 'Whopper Bar' [$] – No Universal Dining Plan. Serves burgers, wraps,

and sandwiches.

Cinnabon [$] – Serves cinnamon rolls and breakfast items.

Cold Stone Creamery [$] – Serves ice cream.

Hot Dog Hall of Fame [$ to $$] – Serves hot dogs.

Lone Palm Airport [$$] – Serves American fare including burgers, sandwiches and a variety of other entrees. This is also a full-service bar.

Menchie's Frozen Yogurt [$] – Serves frozen yogurt.

Moe's Southwest Grill [$] – Serves burritos, tacos, fajitas, and other southwest dishes.

Panda Express [$ to $$] – Serves Chinese food.

Red Oven Pizza Bakery [$ to $$] – Serves pizza and salads. Hands down the best pizza at Universal Orlando.

Starbucks Coffee[$] – Serves coffees, ice-based drinks, sandwiches, and pastries.

Voodoo Doughnuts [$] – Serves luxuriously creative and over-the-top donuts.

Table Service:

Antojitos Authentic Mexican Food [$$ to $$$] – Serves Mexican-style food. Open for dinner only.

Bigfire [$$ to $$$] – Serves pasta, steaks, seafood, chicken and more cooked on an open fire. Open for dinner only.

Bob Marley – A Tribute to Freedom [$$] – Serves Jamaican-style dishes. Open for dinner only.

Bubba Gump Shrimp Co [$$ to $$$] – Serves seafood and other dishes.

The Cowfish Sushi Burger bar [$ to $$] – Serves burgers and sushi.

Hard Rock Cafe Orlando [$ to $$$$] – Serves burgers, steaks, ribs, and other American-style food. Also serves breakfast.

Jimmy Buffet's Margaritaville [$ to $$] – Serves Floridian and Caribbean-inspired food.

NBC Sports Grill & Brew [$ to $$] – Sports-bar style location with 100 TV screens. Serves salads, and American-style food.

Pat O' Briens [$ to $$] – A music venue that serves New Orleans-style dishes.

The Toothsome Chocolate Emporium [$$ to $$$] – A cool Steampunk chocolate factory with full Table Service meals and mouth-watering desserts. Includes a take-out shake counter ($15 to $17 each).

VIVO Italian Kitchen [$ to $$] – Serves Italian food.

Making Reservations:
To make reservations for Table Service restaurants, call (407) 224-3663 or visit opentable.com. Hard Rock Café Orlando priority seating can also be requested online.

Top Tip 1: Most places have happy hours with discounted drinks and snacks. These vary, so ask staff for details.

Top Tip 2: Ask for the free Hard Rock Café VIBE tour and get an insight into the memorabilia and décor of the café. Available daily from 2:00 pm to 9:00 pm; simply ask.

Movie Theater

CityWalk features *Universal Cinemark* with 20 screens, including one that shows films in THX Certified XD (Extreme Digital).

Ticket prices vary according to the time of day and several other factors.

The ticket price for an adult for matinee screenings is $9.50 and goes up to $14 later in the day. Children and seniors pay $8 to $11.

Annual passholders get around $3 off showings at certain times.

There are additional charges for 3D movies.

Mini Golf

Hollywood Drive-In Golf is an adventure golf location with two different courses - one themed to sci-fi *(Invaders from Planet Putt)*, the other themed to horror movies *(The Haunting of Ghostly Greens)*.

The sounds, special effects, lighting, and theming truly immerse you in the miniature world you are in.

Pricing is $20 per adult and $18 per child (ages 3-9). A single course takes between 35 and 45 minutes to complete, with each being made up of 18 holes.

There is a discount for buying tickets to both courses at once - the price is $37 per adult and $33 per child.

The entrance is located next to the *Universal Cinemark* box office.

Discounts for Florida residents, military, seniors, AAA members, and Universal annual pass holders are available.

The location is open from 9:00 am to 2:00 am daily.

Top Tip: Purchase your mini-golf tickets at least one day in advance at hollywooddriveingolf.com and save up to 10% per ticket.

CityWalk Shopping

If you fancy shopping, CityWalk has a few locations to visit including *Quiet Flight Surf Shop,* a large *Universal Studios Store* and the *Universal Legacy Store* (where you can get theme park gear without entering the parks).

Finally, if you are in the mood for some ink, visit *Hart & Huntington TattooCompany.*

Universal's Great Movie Escape

Are you a fan of highly-themed escape rooms? Universal has you covered!

This new addition to CityWalk was added in early 2023 and features a high-tech upgrade to the standard escape room. Puzzles and activities are randomized allowing you to play again and again.

You can choose from an escape room themed to *Jurassic World* or *Back to the Future.* And when we say "room", we don't mean a single room...Universal has stepped this up a notch as each of these two adventures features eight areas with highly detailed sets and "captivating storylines".

In *Jurassic World: Escape*, Universal says: "You've landed a job as a geneticist at a secret lab on Isla Nublar. While undergoing training that includes everything from feeding ferocious dinosaurs to splicing DNA to create new genetic codes, you learn that an apex predator has broken free. Now, you must race against the clock to avoid becoming its prey."

In *Back to the Future: Outatime* "you're transported to a museum in 1993, where you learn that Back to the Future antagonist Biff Tannen has stolen Doc Brown's newest time travel device to sabotage the space-time continuum. Work together to uncover Doc's secret clues as you travel through time, track down Biff, and save the past and the future

before you run 'OUTATIME.'" Each experience starts at $50 plus tax per person, or $300 for a private group experience. Complimentary parking is available for one vehicle per booking.

Each experience lasts around 1 hour and no prior experience of escape rooms is required nor knowing the storyline of either movie. Enjoy!

CityWalk Nightlife

As far as bars and nightclubs are concerned, you will find *Red Coconut Club, Pat O' Briens, CityWalk's Rising Star,* and *Fat Tuesday*.

You will also find live music at *Hard Rock Live Orlando. Lone Palm Airport* is also an outdoor bar just across

from *Jimmy Buffet's*. The cover charge for a single nightclub is $7 - entertainment usually begins at 9:00 pm. *Hard Rock Café* does not have a cover charge.

Top Tip: You can avoid most cover charges before 9:00pm.

For the Little Ones

It may be hard to imagine Universal Orlando as being a place for small kids when rides such as the Velicicoaster and Hollywood Rip Ride Rockit dominate the skyline. Although Universal is not as kid-oriented as Disney's parks, there are still many activities dedicated to children.

....

Before leaving for the Universal Orlando Resort, we recommend you measure your child to avoid them getting excited about attractions they cannot ride.

There is nothing more disappointing than being slightly too short for an attraction they have waited to ride for months; ride operators will not bend the rules, even for half an inch, for everyone's safety. See the minimum height requirements for all attractions on the next page.

Remember that every child has a different comfort zone, and some may well be frightened of an attraction even if they do meet the minimum height requirements. Gently prompting and encouraging them to ride is fine; forcing them is not.

Important: Unlike at the Walt Disney World Resort, baby formula and diapers are not sold at the Universal theme parks.

Universal Studios Florida

Younger members of the family will enjoy seeing Gru and the gang at *Despicable Me: Minion Mayhem* in a 3D simulator ride. There is no minimum height limit in stationary seats. *Minion Blast* is also fun for guests of all ages.

E.T. Adventure can be a little dark in parts but is a relaxing ride – some kids may not enjoy the sensation of flying, however.

The Simpsons Ride also features popular characters. Note that this attraction may be frightening due to the large screen and simulated movements.

The rollercoaster in Dreamworks Land opening in 2024 is a gentle roller coaster for starters. Plus, the other activities opening in Dreamworks Land such as the shows will be kid-friendly.

At the moment Universal does not offer a daytime parade.

Islands of Adventure

Kids will love the *Seuss Landing* area with its play areas, meet and greets, and rides for all ages including the *Caro-Seuss-El; One Fish, Two Fish, Red Fish, Blue Fish*; and *The High in the Sky Seuss Trolley Train Ride.*

In *Toon Lagoon,* you will find several water play areas to splash around in. *Me Ship,*

The Olive is a fun play area here too.

Marvel Super Hero Island also features *Storm Force Accelatron* (an adult must accompany those under 48"/1.22m), this is a themed, more intense teacup ride.

The *Jurassic Park Discovery Center* is also a fun,

educational place to learn about dinosaurs and is open to all ages as it is a walkthrough experience. Camp Jurassic is also a really fun interactive play area for all ages.

For more action-filled rides, try *Pteranodon Flyers, Flight of the Hippogriff*, and *The Amazing Adventures of Spider-Man.*

Ride Height Requirements

Many attractions at Universal Orlando have height requirements for guests' safety. We list all rides with height limits in ascending order, and what park they are in.

No Minimum Height:
• Despicable Me: Minion Blast (no handheld infants)
• Storm Force Accelatron (IOA) - An adult must accompany those under 48" (1.22m)
• One Fish, Two Fish, Red Fish, Blue Fish (IOA) – Children under 48" (1.22m) must ride with an adult

34" (0.87m)
• E.T. Adventure (USF)

36" (0.92m)
• Pteranodon Flyers (IOA) – Guests over 56" must be joined by someone under 36".
• Dreamworks Land Coaster (USF)
• Flight of the Hippogriff (IOA)
• The Cat in the Hat (IOA) – 36" to ride with an adult, or 48" alone
• Skull Island: Reign of Kong (IOA)

40" (1.02m)
• The Amazing Adventures of Spider-Man (IOA)
• Despicable Me: Minion Mayhem
• TRANSFORMERS: The Ride-3D (USF)
• The Simpsons Ride (USF)
• Race Through New York starring Jimmy Fallon (USF)
• The High in the Sky Seuss Trolley Train Ride (IOA) – 40" to ride with an adult, or 48" alone

42" (1.07m)
• MEN IN BLACK: Alien Attack (USF)
• Popeye & Bluto's Bilge-Rat Barges (IOA)
• Jurassic Park River Adventure (IOA)
• Harry Potter and the Escape from Gringotts (USF)

44" (1.12m)
• Dudley Do-Right Ripsaw Falls (IOA)

48" (1.22m)
• Revenge of the Mummy (USF)
• Harry Potter and the Forbidden Journey (IOA)
• Hagrid's Magical Creatures Motorbike Adventure (IOA)

51" (1.29m)
• Hollywood Rip Ride Rockit (USF) – Maximum of 79" (2.00m)
• Jurassic World VelociCoaster (IOA)

52" (1.32m)
• Doctor Doom's Fearfall (IOA)

54" (1.37m)
• The Incredible Hulk Coaster (IOA)

Dining

When visiting Universal Orlando, you will find an abundance of food options, from standard theme park fare to fine dining. However, eating somewhere you have never visited can lead to some uncertainty, especially for picky eaters, so this section is here to help.

....

Refillable Drinks and Popcorn

Popcorn:
Refillable popcorn buckets are a great snack option if you are a big eater. With a refillable popcorn bucket, you pay around $13 for the bucket and then can get as many refills as you want for $2.19 (plus tax) each.

Popcorn refills are only available for regular popcorn; flavored popcorn is not discounted.

You can get your refill at the outdoor popcorn machines at the two parks. There are no refills at *CityWalk*, *Volcano Bay,* or the hotels.

Coca-Cola Freestyle:
Coca-Cola Freestyle is a refillable drinks system. You pay $19 plus tax for a Coca-Cola Freestyle cup. You can then visit any of the Coca Cola Freestyle locations - you will find them inside restaurants and as freestanding machines too - and refill your cup for

free as many times as you want during that day. The cup has an RFID chip that, when activated, allows free refills.

There are over 100 different Coke drink mixes you can choose from at the machines, or you can stick to standard Coke products.

You must wait 10 minutes between dispensing drinks to discourage sharing. Additional days can be added for $11 per day.

Freestyle stations at *CityWalk* and the hotels are separate from this system.

Refillable Souvenir Cups:
Universal sells many souvenir cups in the form of characters (Minions, Simpsons, etc.) or themed (a Butterbeer cup). These cost about $18 each (including one fill) and make for a nice souvenir.

Then, you can visit most Quick Service and Snack locations through the two theme parks and *Volcano Bay* and get refills of sodas, slushies and any non-specialty drink for $1.49, plus tax (e.g. Butterbeer, Pumpkin Juice, and Flaming Moe's are Excluded - Fanta and Coke are included). These cups are valid indefinitely and even on future visits.

For guests on multi-day visits who don't drink a lot of soda, the souvenir cups are likely to work out as better value than Freestyle.

Dining Reservations

When you want to sit down and have a Table Service meal in a busy theme park, you do not want to be kept waiting. Each minute you wait could be used to meet characters, watch shows, or ride attractions. This is where restaurant dining reservations come in.

At Universal, dining reservations are relatively easy to get. Book at http://bit.ly/unireservations.

Except for very busy seasons, you should be able to get a reservation for most restaurants a week or so in advance.

If there is a specific place you want to eat, we recommend you book your table as early as possible.

We have even managed to get same-day reservations, but don't count on it.

Top 5 Table Service Restaurants

Universal has Table Service restaurants dotted across its theme parks, *CityWalk,* and the on-site hotels, and finding the best one can be tough. Luckily, we have rounded up those that you really should not miss.

Note that prices and menus change all the time with seasons and chefs - those listed were correct as of when we last ate at the locations and should be taken as examples only.

1. Mythos (Islands of Adventure) – *Mythos* is often rated as the number one theme park restaurant in all of Orlando, not just Universal. This place is a pure delight to eat in, with its lavishly themed interior, exotic menu, and rather fair prices. This restaurant will truly transport you to a different world.

Entrées are $19 and $38. The food ranges from sandwiches to salmon.

2. Finnegan's Bar and Grill (Universal Studios Florida) – *Finnegan's* is always a fun place to dine, or to go inside for a quick drink. Themed as an Irish Pub, there is a lot of fun to be

had, as well as some delightful treats.

Entrées are $18 to $36. The food includes sandwiches, fish and chips, beef stew, and burgers.

3. Confisco Grille (Islands of Adventure) – Located in the *Port of Entry* area, *Confisco Grille* has a traditional range of theme park food, which may be better for families with younger children or picky eaters. It has a laid-back atmosphere.

Entrées are $17 to $25. You will find ribs, pad thai, sandwiches, salads, nachos, and more on the menu.

4. NBC Sports Grill & Brew (CityWalk) – Many ignore this restaurant when walking past, perhaps discounting it as tacky because of its sports theme. Do not be one of the people who makes that mistake; NBC Sports Grill has some great food on offer and the portions are large!

Entrées are $13 to $21. There is a wide selection of food on offer from wings to flatbreads, nachos, calamari, salads, burgers, pasta, steak, and much

more.

5. Toothsome Chocolate Emporium & Savory Feast Kitchen (CityWalk) – Toothsome is an excellent choice no matter what you feel like eating, and the décor is fun too.

Entrées are $12 to $30. Food ranges from salads to flatbreads, hamburgers, pasta, salmon, and meatloaf.

There is even a dedicated brunch menu featuring crepes, waffles, quiche, and french toast! Brunch items are $11 to $16 each.

MOBILE ORDER

Reduce the time you spend waiting by using Mobile Order on the Universal Orlando app. This free service allowed you to browse menus, choose food and drink items, and pay for your items. You can do this even when not at the restaurant (but you must be in the same park). Upon arrival, tap to confirm you are at the location and pick up your food in minutes.

In certain cases to avoid overcrowding, Mobile Order may be a requirement at certain restaurants. Even if it is not required, we would still recommend it to speed up your visit to dining locations. Mobile Order is available at over 30 locations including at both theme parks, *Volcano Bay*, and *CityWalk*.

Top 5 Quick Service Restaurants

There are times when you may not want a three-course meal, preferring to use the time to watch a show, walk around the parks, or ride your favorite attraction again.

Here are our favorite on-site Quick Service restaurants to make the most of your park time.

1. Three Broomsticks (Islands of Adventure) – Everything about this restaurant puts it at the top spot: the atmosphere, the food, and its opening hours. *Three Broomsticks* is open for breakfast, lunch, and dinner, and is the only fully-fledged restaurant at *The Wizarding World of Harry Potter - Hogsmeade*.

Entrées are $12 to $20. Breakfast entrées come from around the world: England, the USA, and Continental Europe, to name a few locations.

Lunch and dinner revolve around British dishes with some American classics too. You will find pasties, fish & chips, shepherd's pie, as well as smoked turkey legs, rotisserie smoked chicken, and spareribs.

2. Thunder Falls Terrace (Islands of Adventure) – This is another restaurant where the atmosphere adds to the experience. Step foot into *Thunder Falls,* and you are in the middle of the world of Jurassic Park - and you get a spectacular view of the *River Adventure* ride splashdown from the restaurant's huge glass windows.

Entrées are $16.50 to $24.50. On offer are ribs, rice bowls, and rotisserie chicken. The portion sizes are large for theme park meals.

3. Louie's Italian Restaurant (Universal Studios Florida) – As far as pizzas and pasta go inside the theme parks, *Louie's* does it best. It should be noted that there is not a large variety of food on offer at Louie's, and it is not particularly healthy - but it is tasty!

Entrées are $11 to $19. You can also order a full pizza pie to share for $35 to $40.

Food includes spaghetti and meatballs, pizza, sandwiches and fettuccine alfredo. The meatballs and pizzas are the best we've had at a theme park Quick Service location.

4. Leaky Cauldron (Universal Studios Florida) – This location has a great atmosphere inside. Like its other *Wizarding World* companion in this section, you can get some good British grub, including Bangers and Mash, Cottage Pie, Toad in the Hole, Fish and Chips. Entrées are $12 to $18.

5. Croissant Moon Bakery (Islands of Adventure) – The food here is far from your standard theme park fare. This is a bakery and not somewhere to go for a full- blown lunch or dinner meal, but where you might go for breakfast or a snack.

Entrées are $4 to $14.50. Serves continental breakfasts, sandwiches, and great cakes! If you fancy a coffee, this is the place to visit too!

Understanding the Parks

Universal Orlando offers a variety of services designed to ease your day, from photo services to Express Passes, and Single Rider queue lines to package delivery.

My Universal Photos

My Universal Photos is a photo collection system that allows you to get all your in-park photos in one place.

You can get a *My Universal Photos* card from any in-park photographer. Each time you take a photo, hand the photographer this card - they will scan it, and your photos will be grouped.

Before the end of the day, visit one of the *My Universal Photos* stores where you can choose the best pictures and have them printed.

You will need a new *My Universal Photos* card for each day of your vacation unless you purchase a Photo Package. All in-park photos are deleted at the end of the operating day.

Although superficially, the system seems to be reasonably similar to Disney's *Photopass* system, there are not as many in-park photographers (though the number of on-ride photos is impressive).

Photo Package:
The *My Universal Photos* Photo Package is a way to pre-pay for all your in-park photos. When you buy the Photo Package, you will get two *My Universal Photos* cards on a lanyard that you scan any time you have your picture taken in the park.

All these photos are automatically uploaded to the *My Universal Photos* website, where you can later download them.

My Universal Photos includes on-ride photos, character photos, and in-park photographer photos on the same account!

To get a Photo Package, pre-purchase online, visit the *My Universal Photos* stores at the entrance to each park – these are well signposted. Alternatively, after riding an attraction with an on-ride photo, visit the ride's photo desk to purchase the Photo Package.

You can use your Photo Package at the following locations:

Universal Studios Florida:
• On Location (Park Entrance Photos)
• E.T.'s Toy Closet & Photo Spot
• MEN IN BLACK Alien Attack
• Harry Potter and the Escape from Gringotts
• Shutterbutton's Photography Studio (with the Shutterbutton's package)
• Revenge of the Mummy
• Hollywood Rip Ride Rockit
• TRANSFORMERS Photo Op
• The Simpsons Photo Op
• Roaming characters where applicable
• Despicable Me Store Photo Op

Universal's Islands of Adventure:
• DeFotos Expedition Photography (Park Entrance Photos)
• Spider-Man Photo Op in Alterniverse Store
• In-Queue Photo Op at The Amazing Adventures of Spider-Man
• The Incredible Hulk Coaster

• Dudley Do-Right's Ripsaw Falls
• Jurassic Park River Adventure
• Raptor Encounter
• T-Rex Automated Photo Capture in Jurassic Park
• Harry Potter and the Forbidden Journey
• Hagrid's Magical Creatures Motorbike Adventure
• The High In The Sky Seuss Trolley Train Ride! In-Queue Photo Op
• Roaming characters where available
• The Grinch Seasonal Photo Op

There are also 13 locations at *Volcano Bay* including in slides and selfie spots.

Photo Package Pricing:
There are a few different Photo Packages to choose from, depending on how long you visit (prices ex-tax):
• One day – $89.99 online, $109.99 in-park
• Three consecutive days – $109.99 online, and $129.99 in-park
• 30 consecutive days – $139.99, online only
• 1 year – $159.99
• 3-Day Shutterbutton's Photo Package – $159.99

For most visitors, the 3-day package is the best value.

As well as the digital photos obtained via a website, the price of the package also includes discounts on in-park ride photo prints.

The Shutterbutton's Photo Package includes unlimited Digital Downloads for 3 consecutive days and a Shutterbutton's DVD.

Top Tip: To pre-purchase Photo Packages before you go, visit https://presale.amazingpictures.com/UniversalFlorida.aspx. Certain options such as the 1-day and 14-day packages can only be bought online.

Package delivery

Universal Orlando's package delivery service allows you to purchase any item in the park and have it stored until later in the day when you can pick it up. This means you won't have to carry it around all day.

You can choose to have your purchase sent to one of two locations:

• **The front of the park** – At *Volcano Bay*, you pick up your held items at Waturi Marketplace located by the park exit.

At the two theme parks, purchases are sent to the Universal Studios Store located in *CityWalk*.

Allow at least 3 hours for delivery.

• **Your hotel room** – At on-site hotels, you can also have the package delivered to your hotel room (or a collection point at some hotels). It will be delivered the next day between 9:00 am and 4:00 pm. This service is unavailable the day before checkout or the day of checkout itself, so it is only suitable for stays of 3 nights or more.

The Universal Orlando app

The Official Universal Orlando Resort App, available for free on smartphones, allows you to: access wait times for all attractions when inside the parks, get Virtual Line passes, get directions to attractions with step-by-step visual representations, see showtimes and special events, get custom wait time alerts, see park and resort maps, find guest amenities, see park hours, set showtime alerts, share on social media, and locate food items.

You can even buy park tickets and Express Passes right in the app.

Ride Lockers

Many of the rides at Universal do not allow you to take your belongings onto them; loose articles must be placed in lockers.

How to use the in-park ride lockers:

• Approach a locker station. These are near the entrance of all rides that require their use;
• Select 'Rent a locker' from the touch screen;
• Scan your park ticket to be assigned a locker; Keep this ticket with you on the ride to unlock the locker later.
• Go to the locker, put your belongings inside, and press the green button next to the locker to lock the door.

Small lockers are complimentary (14" in width by 5.5" in height by 16.9" in depth / 35.6cm x 14cm x 43cm); these will easily fit purses, wallets, cell phones, Potter wands as well as drinks containers on their side.

Larger lockers, big enough to fit a backpack or a drink standing upright, cost $2.

The small lockers are free for a certain period. This is always longer than the posted wait time. For example, a 90-minute queue for *The Incredible Hulk Coaster* would typically allow you 120 or 150 minutes of locker rental time to allow you to queue, experience the ride, and collect your belongings.

If you keep your belongings in the lockers longer than the free period, charges apply. The cost is $3 for each additional 30 minutes, up to a maximum daily fee of $20.

Lockers for the water rides are not free - they are $4 for a set period (the wait time plus a margin), and $3 for each extra 30 minutes, up to a maximum of $20.

Top Tip 1: If your free locker time expires because the queue line took longer than expected, let a Team Member know and they will help you. There should usually be a Team Member for each ride's lockers.

Top Tip 2: To avoid paying for a water ride locker, you could walk to another ride where lockers are free. *Forbidden Journey* often has long rental times, for example, and would work well for those riding *Jurassic Park: River Adventure* as it is nearby.

Top Tip 3: You don't actually have to use your park ticket on the lockers - any barcode will do. You can also ask for a barcode ticket from a locker attendant. This decreases the chance of you losing your valuable park ticket on the ride.

All-day park locker rentals: All-day, non-ride lockers are available at the entrance to each park – the cost is $12 per day for a standard locker or $15 for a family size locker. You may access these lockers as many times as you want throughout the day, though their non-central location can be a pain. Your best bet is to simply travel light when in the parks.

Universal's Express Pass

Universal Express Pass allows you to skip the majority of the queue lines in both parks for a fee.

The Express Pass is a ticket that allows you to enter a separate shorter attraction queue line with drastically lower wait times. At shows, you enter 15 minutes before guests who do not have an Express Pass so you can get the best seats.

Express Pass access costs between $90 and $380 per person per day - this is in addition to your admission ticket. The pass is complimentary for those staying on-site at *Hard Rock Hotel, Portofino Bay Hotel,* and *Royal Pacific Resort*.

Rides that are not included: Express Passes are valid on all attractions at both theme parks, except *Ollivander's Wand Shop* (both IOA and USF), *Hagrid's Magical Creatures Motorbike Adventure* (as of late 2023), and *Pteranodon Flyers*.

How do I use it? At an attraction entrance, show your Express Pass to the Team Member. They will scan it, and you will be directed to a separate queue line from non-Express Pass guests. Typical waits are 15 minutes or less, even on the busiest days, and are often shorter.

As you will be in a different queue line to the main one, Express Pass guests may lose part of the storyline told in the queue. This is particularly evident at *Revenge of the Mummy,*

TRANSFORMERS, *Harry Potter and the Escape from Gringotts,* and MEN IN BLACK: *Alien Attack.*

The 4 types of Express Pass:
• *Universal Express Pass*: Sold in the parks and online. It allows one ride per participating attraction.
• *Universal Express Unlimited*: Sold online and in the parks. It allows unlimited rides on each participating attraction.
• *Park-To-Park Ticket + Universal Express Unlimited*: Sold online or over the phone (407-224-7840) and includes a regular park admission ticket for both parks and *Universal Express Unlimited* access every day. These tickets are available in one-day or multi-day versions. The ticket expires when all admission days on the ticket are used or 14 days after the first use, whichever is first.
•*On-site Hotel Universal Express Unlimited Pass*: This is a perk for on-site hotel guests staying at the three most expensive hotels. This pass is included for everyone in the hotel room for the whole stay, including the entire check-in and check-out days. It allows unlimited rides on each attraction. A photo of each guest is printed onto this pass.

Each member of your party needs their own Express Pass. If you are not using an *On-site Hotel Universal Express Unlimited Pass* or a *Park-To-Park Ticket + Universal Express Unlimited*, you will need to purchase a separate Express Pass for

each day of your trip. At *Volcano Bay*, Express Pass allows you to skip the Virtual Line once per selected attraction. Hotel Express Passes are not valid at V*olcano Bay* and cost $20 to $150 per day.

Cut the Cost of Express Pass: Guests of select on-site hotels get *Unlimited Express Pass* during their stay, so staying at the *Hard Rock Hotel, Portofino Bay Hotel* or *Royal Pacific Resort* is the best option if you want Express Passes for your entire stay. These are luxury resorts with fantastic amenities, located right next door to the theme parks. Queue-cutting with Express Pass is a bonus!

Take a look at the money you can save: One night at *Royal Pacific Resort* during the busiest season (Holiday) for two adults is $836 with complimentary Hotel Unlimited Express Passes for your entire stay, including check-in and check-out days.

Buying the same Express Passes separately for these days costs $350 per person, per day. For two days, you would be spending $1400 on Express Passes. So, by staying at the *Royal Pacific Resort* you save over $550.

The price gets even better when more people stay in the same room. Even if you don't need the hotel room, it is cheaper to book one, check-in, get your Express Passes and leave straight away.

If you are a family of five, you can get roll-away beds at the on-site hotels for an additional $25 per night, reducing the effective price per person.

Savings are available year-round.

To take advantage of this tip, you should stay at these hotels for one night. Generally, stays longer than one night become poorer value as these hotels are pricey. Two days is usually enough to see everything with Express Pass access! If you want to stay longer, we would suggest spending the other nights at a cheaper hotel.

Do I need an Express Pass?
During peak periods, an Express Pass is almost essential. It *guarantees* you will save hours of waiting. However, Express Passes are expensive and will often double the cost of your

visit.

With careful planning, and by following our touring plans, you can experience most rides without an Express Pass, even during busy seasons.

If you are visiting outside of the peak times of school breaks and holidays, an Express Pass is not as useful.

Outside of peak periods, you often wait less than 20 to 30 minutes for most Attractions with Express Pass.

To do both parks in one day, you *will* need Express Passes.

Finally, if you get an Express Pass, we recommend the 'Unlimited' version. You will want to ride attractions as many times as you wish, not just once each.

If you can't afford it, skip the Express Passes. You will not miss out if you get up early and follow our touring plans (see page 71) – you will wait, but you will save hundreds of dollars too.

Top Tip 1: Do not buy Express Passes in advance unless you are sure the parks will be busy. If unsure, wait until you are at the parks to see the wait times.

Top Tip 2: If buying Express Park tickets at the parks, don't buy them from the kiosk *outside* the park gates – the wait here is usually longer than at other locations *inside* the park.

Top Tip 3: At certain times of the year, there are 'after 4:00 pm' Express Passes on offer at a discounted price. Ask for these, as they are not advertised.

Top Tip 4: The *Park-To-Park Ticket + Universal Express Unlimited* ticket bundle is cheaper than buying park admission and the Unlimited Express Pass separately.

Top Tip 5: The free Hotel Express Pass only applies during regular park hours. During events where a separate admission ticket is required, such as *Halloween Horror Nights*, you will need to buy an event-specific Express Pass. The Hotel Express Pass is also **NOT** valid at *Volcano Bay*.

Stroller and Wheelchair Rentals

Both theme parks offer stroller, wheelchair, and motorized ECV rentals to the left side of each theme park's turnstiles.

Rentals Prices (per day):
• Single Stroller – $15
• Single Kiddie Car – $18
• Double Stroller – $25
• Double Kiddie Car – $28

• Wheelchairs – $12, plus a $50 deposit.
• ECVs – $50, plus a $50 deposit.

The kiddie car is a stroller designed to look like a car with a steering wheel to play with. It features an enclosed front foot area to stop kids slipping out.

ECVs must be operated by a single person aged 18 years old or over.

Wheelchairs can also be rented in the parking rotunda area.

Child Swap

Sometimes when visiting a theme park, two adults want to ride an attraction but have a child who is not tall enough. Universal Orlando has a solution that allows you to take turns riding, but only queue once – Child Swap.

Simply ask a Team Member at an attraction entrance to use Child Swap.

Generally, one or more adults go in the standard queue line while another adult is directed to a Child Swap waiting area.

Once the first group has queued up and ridden the attraction, they proceed to the Child Swap area. Here the first group stays with the child, and the person who sat with the child gets

to ride straight away without having to wait in the queue.

This procedure may vary between attractions and can be combined with Express Pass – ask Team Members at attraction entrances about the specific procedure.

Single Rider

An excellent way to reduce your time waiting in queue lines is to use the Single Rider line instead of the regular queue line.

This is an entirely separate queue that is used to fill free spaces on ride vehicles with guests riding alone. E.g., if a ride vehicle can seat 8 people and a group of 4 turns up, followed by a group of 3, then a guest from the Single Rider queue line will fill the free space on the ride. This makes the wait times shorter for everyone as all spaces on ride vehicles are filled.

Everyone benefits from the system: single riders typically get on much more quickly than the standard wait, and the regular queue line moves marginally quicker as all those single riders aren't in it!

Single Rider (SR) lines may not operate all all times. If the parks are very busy, SR lines can close when the wait in the SR line is the same or greater than the regular line.

If the Single Rider queue line is full and cannot accept more guests, it will also be temporarily closed. If the parks are empty, then sometimes Single Rider lines do not operate either, as there is no need for them.

Some rides have hidden Single Rider lines that are not advertised - in this case, ask the first attraction host you see (usually at attraction entrances) if the Single Rider queue line is open. If it is, then they will direct you accordingly. One example of this is the *Harry Potter and the Forbidden Journey* Single Rider line, which is very easy to miss.

Please note there is no guarantee that the wait in the Single Rider line will be quicker than in the regular standby queue - it often is longer, especially on rides with 2 seats per row such as *VelociCoaster* and *Hagrid's*.

If you are traveling as a group, you can use Single Rider but you *will* ride separately from the others

in your party.

Single Rider lines are available at:
• *The Incredible Hulk*
• *The Amazing Adventures of Spider-Man*
• *Harry Potter and the Forbidden Journey*
• *Jurassic Park River Adventure*
• *Dr. Doom's Fearfall*
• *Dudley Do-Right's Ripsaw Falls*
• *Skull Island: Reign of Kong*
• *Transformers: The Ride*
• *Hollywood Rip Ride Rockit*
• *Revenge of the Mummy*
• *Harry Potter and the Escape from Gringotts*
• *Hagrid's Magical Creatures Motorbike Adventure*
• *Jurassic World: VelociCoaster*

Guests with Disabilities

Visiting a theme park can be a complicated process for guests with disabilities but Universal Orlando has worked hard to give people in this situation as much of the full theme park experience as possible. Although we cannot cover every kind of disability in this section, we have tried to include as much information as possible.

Universal Attraction Assistance Pass

The below system was introduced in summer 2023 and will differ if you have visited previously.

How to get an Attraction Assistance Pass:
1) Visit accessibilitycard.org at least 48 hours before arriving for your vacation and register for an IBCCES Individual Accessibility Card (IAC) using the online application form. You will need to provide personal information, a recent photo, and documentation showing your needs or accessibility support.

2) Once your online application is approved, a Universal Team Member will contact you to discuss your request for an attraction queue accommodation.

3) If deemed necessary, Universal will offer you an Attraction Assistance Pass to use throughout your visit.

Examples of Needs or Accommodations Requests for the IAC:
• Cannot stand in line for a long period of time
• Requires ride harness or other supports
• Sensory sensitivities
• Wheelchair access
• Physical or mobility restrictions
• Require visual assistance or guidance
• Special dietary needs

Please note that not all the above accommodations will allow you access to an Attraction Assistance Pass. These are given out at Universal Orlando's discretion.

Using the Attraction Assistance Pass:
When you reach an attraction you would like to ride, show your Attraction Assistance Pass to the Team Member at the ride entrance.

If the wait time is less than 30 minutes, you will be immediately directed towards an alternative queue; this is often the Express Pass queue line.

If the attraction's wait time is at least 30 minutes, then the Team Member will write down a time on your Pass to return – we will call this a 'reservation' in this section.

When your reservation time comes around, show your pass at the ride entrance to be granted entry through the alternative queue. This is NOT a front-of-the-line ticket and waits can still be up to 15 minutes per ride.

You can only hold one ride 'reservation' at any time.

You may still enjoy accelerated entrance to attractions with less than a 30-minute wait, even with an active reservation.

If you want to change which attraction you have a reservation for, visit the next attraction and make a reservation with the attraction's greeter at the entrance. This will void your previous reservation.

An Assistance Pass allows up to 25 reservations; this is more than enough for a single day.

The Assistance Pass is valid for up to 6 people in the person's party.

Other Assistance for Disabled Guests

Deaf/Hard of Hearing – For guests who are deaf or hard of hearing, you may request American Sign Language interpretation for in-park shows by emailing SignLanguageServices@universalorlando.com at least 2 weeks before arrival.

Closed captioning and assistive listening devices, guidebooks for guests with disabilities, and attraction scripts are also available at Guest Services in each theme park.

Mobility Impairment and Wheelchairs – The whole of Universal Orlando has been designed to be as wheelchair and stroller-accessible as possible with ramps instead of steps. All the shopping and dining facilities are accessible. Guests who would like to use a stroller as a wheelchair should ask for a special tag from Guest Services.

Outdoor stage shows also have designated areas for wheelchair users and their parties.

Most rides are accessible –

most will require a transfer; some may allow you to ride in your wheelchair.

You can get a wheelchair at the parking rotunda to help with the considerable distance from the rotunda to the theme parks – simply ask the Team Members here. You can also rent a wheelchair inside the theme parks.

If using a parking rotunda wheelchair, guests may pay the additional cost for an ECV once at the parks or use this wheelchair throughout the day.

You do not NEED to have an Attraction Assistance Pass if you are in a wheelchair as all rides have an accessible entrance, but it can make things easier when there are particularly long queues, so we do recommend it.

If you, or someone you are with, have a disability that is not visible, we thoroughly recommend the use of the Assistance Pass – without one you will need to use the regular queue line.

By its nature as a water park, accessibility at *Volcano Bay* is very limited for rides - you must be able to transfer from a wheelchair to the ride vehicle or slides and be able to climb many steps for most rides. ECVs are not permitted in queues or on rides.

Service Animals are permitted throughout the theme parks, but each attraction will have a specific way of boarding. Portable kennels are available at some attractions for service animals. The Team Members at the entrance of each attraction can provide more information.

Special restrictions apply to guests with prosthetic limbs and guests with oxygen tanks.

Rides and shows: More information about rides and shows is available in the Riders Guide for Rider Safety & Guests with Disabilities (PDF file). It can be downloaded online at http://bit.ly/uordisability.

Tips, Savings and More

This section covers various ways to make your trip better - from ways to save time and money to Early Park Admission and character meets.

Money Saving Tips

Take food with you
Universal allows you to bring your own food into the parks. Whether it is a bag of chocolates or a drink, you can purchase these items at a fraction of the price anywhere outside of Universal property.

For drinks, why not put them in a cooling bag (hard-sided coolers are not allowed in the parks), or freeze them to drink throughout the day. Food should be fine in a backpack throughout the day.

Glass containers and bottles are not permitted in the parks.

Bring rain gear
There is a high likelihood that at some point during your Universal Orlando theme park adventure you will get wet, whether it is on one of the water rides, or in one of the famous Floridian thunderstorms.

Either way, we recommend you bring rain protection from home - either a raincoat, a poncho, or even an umbrella (beware of lightning and umbrellas).

This saves you 1) from purchasing these items in the theme parks at inflated prices, and 2) wearing wet clothes when you get soaked.

Those human-sized dryers outside the water rides that you can pay $5 to go into are not very effective – don't waste your money.

Buy tickets in advance
Do not buy tickets at the gate – you will waste time and pay more than you need to.

There is no excuse not to buy your tickets in advance. You can do this over the phone, online at universalorlando.com, or through a third party. You will save at least $20 per multi-day ticket by pre-purchasing them.

Also, some countries can get exclusive deals, such as the UK, where there is a 14-day ticket for at a discount on the official UK Universal Orlando website.

You do not NEED an Express Pass
By following our Touring Plans, you will be able to see the majority of the attractions at both Universal theme parks in two days. If you have two full days, an Express Pass is not a must: you can save up to $350 per person on Express Passes alone through planning.

If you want to do everything in one day, Express Passes are a must-have.

If you want Express Passes, stay on-site at certain hotels
The on-site hotels are more expensive than those off-site, but staying at the top-tier on-site hotels gets you unlimited Express Passes for everyone in the room for the duration of your stay, including check-in and check-out days. To make the most of this, book a one-night stay at a Universal hotel.

On your check-in day, despite the fact your room may only be available from 4:00 pm onwards, you can check-in at any time, leave your bags and get your Express Passes. This means you can arrive at 7:00 am or 8:00 am, check-in, and head straight to the parks.

On your check-out day, your Express Passes are valid until theme park closing, even after you check out. Express Passes are included with rooms at the *Hard Rock Hotel, Royal Pacific Resort,* and *Portofino Bay Resort.*

Stay off-site
If you are on a budget, then stay off-site. There are many hotels just off Universal Orlando Resort property – a two to three-minute drive away or a 15-minute walk.

These rooms can cost a fraction of the price of the on-site hotels. Plus, many do not have a nightly parking fee.

Loyalty cards
AAA members, American Express Cardholders, and UK-based AA members all receive discounts throughout the resort. The AAA/AA discount is usually around 10% at restaurants and shops - ask for it any time you pay.

Ride photos
Universal is pretty strict on you not taking photos of the monitors showing your on-ride pictures.

As such, we recommend purchasing a *My Universal Photos* – see page 56 for more on this. It will pay for itself if you plan on buying just a few ride photos.

Stay at a partner hotel
Stay at one of Universal Orlando's partner hotels to receive in-room coupons. You may get Early Park Admission too.

Free lockers
Universal charges for lockers on water rides but not on any other rides. Simply walk to a non-water ride and use those lockers.

However, you must be prepared to do a lot of walking to save a few dollars. Also, be ready to search for the ride with the longest wait times to store your belongings.

Harry Potter and the Forbidden Journey often has lockers with long access Times, for example.

Operating Hours and Ride Closures

The Universal Orlando Resort is open 365 days a year and park operating hours vary according to demand.

On days when more visitors are expected, the parks are open longer; when there aren't so many visitors, the parks close earlier. The parks always operate for their advertised operating hours.

We strongly advise that you check opening hours in

advance of your visit. Hours may change closer to the date of your visit, so do re-check.

Park operating hours can be verified up to two months in advance at bit.ly/unihours.

Ride refurbishments also happen throughout the year to keep rides operating safely and efficiently, and rides and attractions close throughout the year to be renewed.

Generally speaking, refurbishments tend to avoid the busier times of the year.

Ride closures are only published a month or so in advance on the same page as the opening hours.

Remember that rides may close for technical issues or weather reasons. There is no reason to be angry at the ride attendants, as they do not control whether the ride runs or not.

How to Spend Less Time Waiting In Line

Park opening
Make sure you get to the theme park well before it officially opens. Ideally, you should be at the gates 30 minutes or more before opening. Remember it will take some time to park if you driving to the resort.

Early morning is the least busy time, and in the first hour, you can usually ride 3 or 4 of the biggest attractions - something that takes several hours during the rest of the day.

The parks often open earlier than advertised, particularly during busy periods.

Use Single Rider lines
If you do not mind riding separately from the rest of your party, use the Single Rider queue lines. See page 61 for more on these. They reduce your wait time significantly so that you can experience more each day; these are available at a surprisingly large number of major attractions.

Touring Plans
We have created expertly designed touring plans that tell you what order to ride the attractions in; these let you see as much as possible. See page 71.

The 59-minute rule
If Universal closes its parks at 9:00pm, that is when the queue lines (not the rides) close. Anyone in the queue line at park closing time is allowed to ride, no matter how long the wait is. If you have one final ride to do and it is getting to park closing time, get into the queue line before the park closes, and you will still be able to ride.

This rule may not apply if an attraction has an exceptionally long wait time that would cause it to keep running for hours after the published closing time.

Character Meet and Greets

Meeting characters can be one of the most enjoyable parts of the day in a theme park. At Universal Orlando, there are many characters to meet, and they usually have little-to-no queues.

At *Marvel Superhero Island*, you will usually find Captain America, Dr. Doom, The Green Goblin, Spider-Man, Storm, and Wolverine. They even make their appearances (and disappearances) on cool quad bikes a lot of the time.

You can also meet the Seuss characters at *Seuss Landing,* including Cat in the Hat, The Grinch, and Thing 1 and 2!

At *Universal Studios Florida,* you will find the characters from The Simpsons including Bart, Lisa, Homer, Marge, Krusty the Clown, and Sideshow Bob.

You will also find the Blues Brothers, the Men in Black, SpongeBob, the Minions and Gru, and the Transformers characters regularly in areas outside their respective attractions.

Other characters also make appearances such as Scooby-Doo and Shaggy, Lucy Ball, Woody Woodpecker, Betty Boop, and Marilyn Monroe.

Character schedules are on your park map. Some are not listed there, so check for appearances in the parks' Character Zones, located near the park entrance at *Universal Studios Florida*, and in *Toon Lagoon* at *Islands of Adventure*.

Early Park Admission

How about getting into the theme parks before other guests? Benefit from shorter queue lines at select attractions, and extra ride time, with Universal's Early Park Admission (EPA).

During most of the year, Universal Orlando Resort offers one hour's early entry to one of the two theme parks, plus *Volcano Bay*. At peak times this may be available at both parks.

This benefit is available to on-site hotel guests and guests who have booked a Universal Vacation Package. It is available daily, including check-in and check-out days.

At *Islands of Adventure,* you will be able to access *The Wizarding World of Harry Potter: Hogsmeade,* including all attractions (except *Hogwarts Express,* which opens when *Universal Studios Florida* starts its operating day), as well as *Jurassic World VelociCoaster.*

At *Universal Studios Florida*, you can access *The Wizarding World of Harry Potter: Diagon Alley* and its attractions, minus the *Hogwarts Express*, which opens at the same time as *Universal's Islands of Adventure. Despicable Me: Minion Mayhem* is also available for Early Park Admission.

Early entry is offered daily for on-site hotel guests. Early Park Admission is also offered with Vacation

Packages booked through Universal whether staying on-site or not, as long as you have booked through Universal and purchased accommodation and park tickets together.

The park which is open for Early Park Admission is announced in advance on the Universal Orlando website. This may change as your trip approaches. During peak periods, both parks may be open - during less busy periods only one of the two parks is open.

In all cases, *Volcano Bay* is open for early admission in addition to the theme park(s) where seven of the top attractions are open.

How do I get Early Park Admission?
Guests staying at Universal on-site hotels show their room key to gain early admission to the parks.

If using this on your arrival date, make sure to check in before Early Admission starts and then over to the parks; your room will not be ready, but you will have Early Admission privileges. You may be sent a text

message with your room number later on. If you do not receive it, stop by the front desk to get your room number.

Guests with a Universal Vacation Package staying off-site do not need to check in to their hotel room. Simply go straight to the Will Call kiosks located by the entrance to each park.

Here you can enter your confirmation number given to you when booking to redeem your tickets with Early Park Admission.

We advise you to bring your travel confirmation sent to you when you booked the package. This proves that you are entitled to this benefit in case there are any problems at the turnstiles.

Early entry is one hour before regular park opening – that is 8:00 am most of the year (with the theme parks opening for regular guests at 9:00 am), and 7:00 am during peak seasons. *Volcano Bay*'s Early Park Admission is usually 8:00am or 9:00am.

Seasonal Events

Universal Orlando offers something different all year round. Whether it is live entertainment, horror mazes, or Holiday cheer, the resort has it all covered.

Rock the Universe
January 26th to 28th 2024

Rock the Universe is a whole weekend dedicated to Christian faith and worship, with Christian rock music.

As well as the main stage with Christian acts, the FanZone has more live music, as well as band autograph sessions, karaoke, and the attractions are open too. On Saturday night, guests can enjoy the Candle-lighting Ceremony.

There is also a free Sunday Morning Worship Service led by a guest speaker for those with *Rock the Universe* tickets. Select attractions also operate.

Rock the Universe is a separately ticketed event that operates outside of regular park hours. 2024 tickets are $80 for one night or $120 for both nights.

For $196 guests could enjoy both event nights plus admission to the parks for three days with park-to-park access. For $151, you could get the same, but with access to one park per day. These are fantastic value.

Top Tip: A one-night event-only Express Pass was $30 for one use per participating attraction, or $40 for unlimited uses.

Mardi Gras
2024 dates unconfirmed. Took place in 1st Feb to 16th Apr in 2023.

Celebrate New Orleans with Universal's Mardi Gras. Mardi Gras is included with regular park admission.

The Mardi Gras Parade has colorful floats and joyous music. Enjoy the traditional throwing of the beads from the floats. The parade takes place on select dates during Mardi Gras.

The Music Plaza stage hosts live acts on select nights. The lineup in the past has included Macklemore, Sean Paul, Pitbull, and others. Concerts are standing-room only.

There are also New Orleans

Bands in the French Quarter Courtyard and stalls with local cuisine, including jambalaya and gumbo.

After the parks shut, head to *CityWalk's* bars and clubs

for more New Orleans fun.

Top Tip: When the parade starts, the regular shows and attractions at the park cease operating.

Halloween Horror Nights

2024 dates unconfirmed. 1st Sep to 4th Nov in 2023.

Halloween Horror Nights is an evening extravaganza with heavily-themed scare mazes (a.k.a. haunted houses), live shows, and scare zones where "scare-actors" roam around frightening guests. The theming is second to none. *Halloween Horror Nights* has been running for over 30 years.

Universal warns the event "may be too intense for young children and is not recommended for children under the age of 13". No costumes or masks are allowed at the event. There is no trick-or-treating here; the idea is to scream.

Halloween Horror Nights (HHN) is very popular, and *Universal Studios Florida* gets extremely crowded during this event.

On the busiest nights, you can expect to wait 90 minutes or longer in line for each haunted house. Therefore, we highly recommend you purchase an HHN Express Pass for the full experience and to see everything. Even with Express Passes, waits can regularly reach an hour. You will likely need several visits to see everything without Express Passes.

When is HHN?
Although 2024 event dates had not been announced at the time of publishing, dates are broadly similar every year. The event runs on select nights from early September to early November.

What is part of HHN?
Most years there are around ten scare mazes. For example, 2023 included both original houses and franchises such as *Chucky* and *The Last of Us*. Guests can expect each house to last 3 to 5 minutes. Plus, there were 5 scare zones with roaming characters in 2023.

As far as shows, 2023 saw just one called *Nightmare Fuel Revenge Dream*. In the past there has also been a nighttime spectacular on the *USF* lake, featuring projections, water screens, and fountains. This was not present in 2023 but could return in future.

The following attractions were also open during HHN in 2023 and are part of the typical line-up each year: *TRANSFORMERS The Ride 3D, Hollywood Rip Ride Rockit, MEN IN BLACK Alien Attack, Revenge of the Mummy,* and *Harry Potter and the Escape from Gringotts*.

Queues for rides are generally very short throughout the event. Guests with a HHN Express Pass can use it for both the scare mazes and the rides.

Is Diagon Alley part of HHN?
Sort of. For the first time ever, in 2023, the Death Eaters roamed around Diagon Alley as a form of light scare zone. You could interact with them but they weren't expressly there to scare you - more to create a creepy vibe. The rest of the

area was open in its normal state with *Escape from Gringotts*, the shops and the eateries open making this a relatively safe refuge from the scares.

Pricing:
Tickets for 2024 are not yet on sale. For reference, in 2023, a single admission ticket to HHN cost $85 to $130 depending on the date of your visit. There are many other ticket options.

HHN as an add-on:
You can also add one night of *Halloween Horror Nights* to your daytime park ticket and save money (versus purchasing each separately). Your *HHN* ticket does not have to be used on the same day as your park ticket.

Multi-night Tickets:
For online purchases, the *Rush of Fear* pass was great value at $180. It allowed entry to every *HHN* night during September for one price. A *Rush of Fear + HHN Express Pass* option was also available that allowed you entry during September and to bypass the regular lines once at each of the houses every night – this was $530.

Other multi-day ticket options exist for selected dates in September and October, and even for every HHN date. These were priced at $230 to $920, depending on the dates and if they included Express Pass.

HHN Express Passes:
In 2023, these cost $180 to $250 per person per night and were valid during the event for haunted houses and attractions. These often sell out.

On peak nights, you *need* an HHN Express Pass to see everything, as wait times for houses are typically 90 minutes to 3 hours. Even with an Express Pass, you may have to wait an hour or longer to enter the houses on peak nights. Express Passes purchased for daytime at Universal Orlando are not valid during HHN, nor are the Hotel Express Passes.

RIP Tours:
RIP guided tours are Universal's 'VIP' experience. These offer one-time immediate access to each house, plus the attractions, is $380 to $450 per person, plus event admission. A private option costs extra.

Daytime Guided Tours:
To see how the HHN horror is created without scares, take the *Unmasking the Horror Tour*. This is a daytime lights-on walk through 3 haunted houses with a guide. You'll learn about the creative process without the scares. Tours are $90 to $150 per person. Each tour goes through different houses – to see all six, it's $170 to $220 per person.

The Holiday Season and Grinchmas

Mid-November to early January

The Holiday season is filled with fun and magic. This information is for 2023 as 2024 info is not out yet - the event is very similar each year.

Thanksgiving
The parks do not hold Thanksgiving events apart from meals. The on-site hotels offer buffets, and character meets.

Christmas
At *Universal Studios Florida*, *Universal's Holiday Parade featuring Macy's* rolls through the streets with floats from the Thanksgiving Day Parade in New York City. This event runs daily.

Mannheim Steamroller, the biggest-selling Christmas band of all time, rocks the stage on select dates. This is included in your regular admission.

At *Islands of Adventure*, *Grinchmas Who-liday Spectacular* is a show with The Grinch, retelling how he

stole Christmas. There is also The Grinch & Friends Character Breakfast on select dates (from $59 per adult, $33 per child).

Hogsmeade and *Diagon Alley* are transformed by festive décor and unique entertainment. A stunning projection show wraps Hogwarts Castle in spectacular holiday spirit.

Finally, you can enjoy the Universal's Holiday Tour with Grinch greetings, reserved show seating, food, an after-hours showing of *The Magic of Christmas* at Hogwarts Castle and much more. Pricing is $80-$120 per person.

There are no meets with Santa Claus at either park. On-site hotels have holiday dining, tree-lightings, live music, Hanukkah candle lightings, visits from Santa, and Holiday movies.

New Year's Eve
In previous years, *CityWalk* has hosted a ticketed New Year's Eve party event with admission to party zones, a pyrotechnics display, food, a champagne toast and more. Tickets ran at $120. Over 21s only. A VIP package was $195.

Hard Rock Orlando hosts its own NYE party.

The theme parks are open late for New Year's Eve too. The hotels host parties with food, DJs and more.

Keep an eye on UniversalOrlando.com to check which elements will return this year.

Touring Plans

To make the most of your time at the parks, we highly recommend you follow one of our touring plans. These touring plans are not designed for you to have a leisurely, slow day through the parks; they are designed for you to see and do as much as possible, while still having a lot of fun.

....

How to use our Touring Plans

Due to the way our touring plans are designed, you will often need to cross the park back and forth to save you from waiting in long queue lines, but ultimately this extra walking means you can get the most out of your Universal Orlando Resort experience.

Generally speaking, our touring plans have you riding the most popular attractions (with the longest waits) at the start and end of the day when they are less busy. During the middle of the day, you will visit the attractions that have consistent wait times, and watch shows. This maximizes your time.

Touring with Express Pass:
These touring plans presume you do not have Express Pass access. If you do have this, then you are free to explore the park in whatever order you want, as you won't have to worry about waiting a long time for each attraction.

The exception is *Hagrid's Magical Creatures Motorbike Adventure*, which at the moment does not have Express Pass access - wait times are long for this all day, so either do it first or last.

Touring without Express Pass:
As the Universal Orlando theme parks do not have an abundance of attractions, wait times can be long throughout both parks. It is, however, entirely possible to do all the rides in a single park on the same day with some planning.

We recommend you spend at least one day at each theme park and then use a third or fourth day to re-do your favorite attractions at both parks, as well as any others you may have missed.

The key to making the most of these touring plans is to arrive at the park before it opens; this means being at the parking garages at least about 60 minutes before

park opening if you are driving in. The parking garages open 90 minutes before the first park opens.

If you want to buy tickets on the day, you will need to be at the park gates at least 45 minutes before opening.

Otherwise, make sure to be at the park gates at least 30 minutes before opening with your park admission in hand. This is because the parks regularly open up to 30 minutes earlier than the advertised opening time.

Using our Touring Plans:
Follow the steps in order. If there is a particular attraction you do not wish to experience, skip that step, and then follow the next one - do not change the order of the steps.

1-Day Plan for Universal Studios Florida

Note: If you have Early Park Admission into *Universal Studios Florida*, you should ride the *Minion Mayhem* ride (which is open as a bonus!), then explore the *WWOHP*, then follow this plan.

Step 1: Get to the turnstiles with your park ticket in hand at least 30 minutes before the advertised park opening time. Proceed through the gates. Grab a park map and head towards *Despicable Me: Minion Mayhem*. Ride it. If the wait is longer than 30 minutes, we will skip this ride as the time you lose here really impacts the rest of your day.

Step 2: Experience *TRANSFORMERS: The Ride*. There is a Single Rider line. If you find that the wait is long, skip this step and ride *TRANSFORMERS* at the end of the day.

Step 3: Ride *Hollywood Rip Ride Rockit*. There is a Single Rider line available, though it moves slowly. At this time of the day, the regular standby queue line should not be too long.

Step 4: Ride *Revenge of the Mummy*. A Single Rider line is available. We recommend the standard queue for the theming. Wait times rarely exceed 45 minutes.

Step 5: Experience *The Simpsons Ride*.

Step 6: Ride *Men in Black:*

Alien Attack. A Single Rider line is available, which usually moves very quickly.

Step 7: Have a Quick Service lunch to maximize your time.

Step 8: Let's ride something gentle after lunch. Ride *E.T. Adventure*. Waits are usually less than 30 minutes.

Step 9: Watch *Universal's Horror Make-Up Show*. This is our favorite live show. The theater is relatively small, so arrive about 20 minutes before the performance is due to start to be guaranteed a seat.

Step 10: Experience *Despicable Me: Minion Blast*.

Step 11: Experience *Race Through New York Starring Jimmy Fallon*.

Step 12: Experience *Fast and Furious: Supercharged*. Alternatively, watch *The Bourne: Stuntacular* - do

both, if they are of interest.

Step 13: Head to *The Wizarding World of Harry Potter: Diagon Alley*. You want to enter *Diagon Alley* at least 3 hours before the park closes. Crowds are lightest at the end of the day. Ride *Harry Potter and the Escape from Gringotts*, followed by a return journey on the *Hogwarts Express* (a Park-to-Park ticket is required to ride this). If you have the time, experience *Ollivander's Wand Shop*.

Note: We do not include all park attractions here due to time constraints. For example, those opening in the new Dreamworks Land in 2024 will be of limited interest to most guests, except the very youngest.

If you have no interest in *The Wizarding World of Harry Potter*, it is easily possible to every other attraction in the park in one day.

1-Day Plan for Islands of Adventure

Step 1: Arrive at the park entry turnstiles with your ticket at least 30 minutes before opening. Go through the *Port of Entry* area.

Step 2:
Option A - If you *have* Early Park Admission, ride *Hagrid's Magical Creatures Motorbike Adventure* first before continuing this plan from step 3.

Option B - If you *do not* have Early Park Admission and the park is offering this perk on this day, ride *Jurassic World: VelociCoaster* first and then continue from step 3.

Option C - If there is *no* Early Park Admission at this park on this day for *any guests*, ride *Hagrid's* first, then continue from step 3.

Step 3: Ride *The Amazing Adventures of Spider-Man*.

Step 4: Ride *The Incredible Hulk Coaster*.

Step 5: Ride *Dr. Doom's Fearfall*.

Step 6: You should have done this within the first 90 minutes. Now, choose either kids' rides (Step 7 to 10) or water rides (Step 11).

Step 7: Ride *The Cat in the Hat* in *Seuss Landing*.

Step 8: Ride *One Fish, Two Fish, Red Fish, Blue Fish*.

Step 9: Head to *Seuss Landing* and ride the *High in the Sky Seuss Trolley Train Ride*.

Step 10: Ride the *Caro-seuss-el*. The wait is usually less than 10 minutes.

Step 11: Head to *Toon Lagoon* and do the three water rides. *Dudley's Do-Right's Ripsaw Falls* should be first, followed by *Popeye & Bluto's Bilge-Rat Barges*, and finally *Jurassic Park River Adventure*.

Step 12: Lunch. Save time with a Quick Service meal. Eat outdoors, away from the A.C. if you have done the water rides.

Step 13: If you fit the limited ride requirements, ride *Pteranodon Flyers*. This will likely be one of the longest waits of the day.

Step 14: Ride *Skull Island: Reign of Kong*.

Step 15: Now only a few minor rides remain, as well as *The Wizarding World of Harry Potter (WWOHP)*. If there are at least 4 hours until park closing, follow the next steps. If there are less than m4 hours, head to step number 18.

Step 16: Explore *Camp Jurassic*.

Step 17: Ride *Storm Force Accelatron*.

Step 18: Head to WWOHP. Ride *Hagrid's Magical Creatures Motorbike Adventure*.

Step 19: Experience *Ollivander's Wand Shop*. If you are visiting *Universal Studios Florida*, skip this as they have an *Ollivander's* with shorter waits.

Step 20: Ride *Flight of the Hippogriff*.

Step 21: Ride *Harry Potter and the Forbidden Journey*.

Step 22: Depending on which you haven't yet done, ride *Jurassic World VelociCoaster* or *Hagrid's Magical Creatures Motorbike Adventure* to round off the day. As long as you are in line before the park closes, Universal will let you experience the ride.

Top Tip: A common theme park trick is to post inflated wait times during the last operating hour to trick you into not queuing up for rides. Use your judgment. If the park is less busy now than it was in the middle of the day, then the actual wait times will be much shorter.

Best of Both Parks in 1-Day Touring Plan

In this touring plan, we show you how to hit the biggest attractions in both parks. It is not feasible to do *all* the attractions at both parks in just one day, so we have only included the highlights. This is a fast-paced plan.

You will need a Universal Orlando Park-to-Park ticket to access both parks on the same day.

Note: If you have Early Park Access at *Universal Studios Florida*, ride *Despicable Me*, then *Escape from Gringotts* first, and then hop on the *Hogwarts Express* to *Islands of Adventure* and pick up the plan below.

Step 1: Arrive at the park entry turnstiles of *Islands of Adventure* with your ticket at least 30 minutes before opening. Walk through the *Port of Entry* area.

Step 2: Head straight to *Hagrid's Magical Creatures Motorbike Adventure* and ride it. Use Single Rider to save time.

Step 3: Ride *The Amazing Adventures of Spider-Man*. Use Single Rider to save time.

Step 4: Ride *The Incredible Hulk Coaster*. Use Single Rider to save time.

Step 5: Ride *Jurassic World: Velicicoaster*. This will likely be the longest wait of the day. Don't bother with Single Rider here as it typically doesn't make much of a difference.

Step 6: Have lunch in the *WWOHP*.

Step 7: Ride *Harry Potter and the Forbidden Journey*.

Step 8: Take the *Hogwarts Express* to *Universal Studios Florida*.

Step 9: Enter *WWOHP: Diagon Alley* and ride *Escape from Gringotts*. Use Single Rider to save time.

Step 10: Ride *Revenge of the Mummy*. Use Single Rider to save time.

Step 11: Experience *TRANSFORMERS: The Ride*. Use the Single Rider line to save time.

Step 12: Ride *The Simpsons Ride*.

Step 13: Ride *Hollywood Rip Ride Rockit*.

If time still remains, have dinner somewhere in the *Wizarding World* and enjoy some of the wand experiences if you have purchased an interactive wand. If there is any other attraction or show you'd like to experience, do so now.

Important: By leaving a major ride until the end of the day, there is always the risk that you may not be able to ride if it breaks down.

Special Thanks

Thank you very much for reading *The Independent Guide to Universal Orlando 2024*. We hope this travel guide makes a big difference to your vacation and you have found some tips to save you time, money, and hassle. Be sure to check out the next three pages with our exclusively commissioned maps.

Please leave us a review online to support us - they make a huge difference!

If you have enjoyed this guide you may want to check out other books from the author:
• The Independent Guide to Disneyland Paris
• Amazing London Walks

Have fun at the Universal Orlando Resort!

Photo credits:
The following photos have been used in this guide under a Creative Commons Attribution 2.0 license:
Universal Globe - Alison Sanfacon; Photos of all on-site hotels, Hollywood Rip Ride Rocket, Jimmy Fallon, Fast and Furious, Shrek 4-D, Cabana Bay Bus, Reign of Kong, Spider-Man ride and character photo, Nightlife/Rising Star, CityWalk Dining/Cowfish, Antojitos, Quick Service photo, Tri-Wizard Tournament, Aventura Hotel, Cinematic Spectacular, Rock the Universe, Universal's Great Movie Escape, Refillable Mug and Mardi Gras - Universal Orlando; Men in Black, Woody Woodpecker's Nuthouse Coaster, One Fish Two Fish, Storm Force Accelatron, Pteranodon Flyers and Single Rider - Jeremy Thompson; Animal Actors on Location, Planning/Staff and Express Pass, Character Meets with Sideshow Bob - Theme Park Tourist; Chad Sparks - Hogwarts Express; Diagon Alley - osseus; Nintendo Logo - Nintendo Co., Ltd; Volcano Bay - Paulo Guereta; Diagon Alley - amyr_81; Height requirements - Theme Park Tourist; Aventura Hotel, New York City streets and Sapphire Falls- RainO975; Despicable Me - simon17964; Gringotts - Chris Favero; Hagrid's Motorbike Adventure - Rain097; Endless Summer Resort - .Martin.; CityWalk - Theme Park Tourist; Mini Golf image - wanderland.xyzl; - Universal Orlando.

Cover Images: Velocicoaster - wanderland.xyz; Jurassic Park Arch - Dave Harwood; Mel's Drive-In - Caroline Cagnin; Wizarding World (front)- Junchen Zhou; Universal panorama - Mikhail Nilov; Trident and waterfront- rafaelsamir; Kings Cross - mmdexe;

HARRY POTTER, characters, names, and related indicia are trademarks of © Warner Bros. Entertainment Inc. Harry Potter Publishing Rights and © JKR.

Universal Studios Florida Map

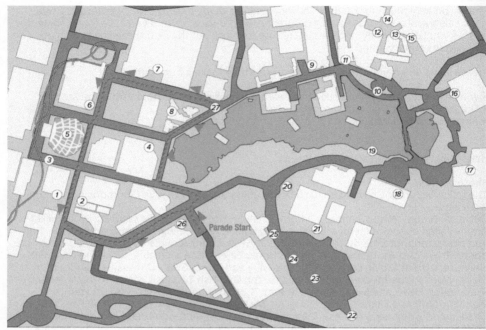

MINION LAND
1. Despicable Me: Minion Mayhem (Express)
2. Despicable Me: Minion Blast (Express)

PRODUCTION CENTRAL
3. Hollywood Rip Ride Rockit (Express)
4. 'TRANSFORMERS' The Ride: 3D (Express)
5. Music Plaza Stage
6. Race Through New York Starring Jimmy Fallon (Express)

NEW YORK
7. Revenge of the Mummy (Express)
8. The Blue Brothers Show

SAN FRANCISCO
9. Fast and Furious: Supercharged (Express)

THE WIZARDING WORLD OF HARRY POTTER - DIAGON ALLEY
10. The Knight Bus
11. Hogwarts Express - King's Cross Station (Express)
12. Knockturn Alley
13. Ollivanders
14. Harry Potter and the Escape from Gringotts (Express)

15. Live Performance Stage

WORLD EXPO
16. Fear Factor Event Stage
17. MEN IN BLACK: Alien Attack (Express)
18. The Simpsons Ride (Express)
19. Kang & Kodos' Twirl & Hurl (Express)

KIDZONE AND DREAMWORKS LAND
20. New Attraction Coming in 2024
21. New Attraction Coming in 2024
22. New Attraction Coming in 2024
23. New Dreamworks Coaster Coming in 2024 (Express)
24. New Attraction Coming in 2024
25. E.T. Adventure (Express)

HOLLYWOOD
26. Universal Orlando's Horror Make-Up Show (Express)

ENTERTAINMENT
Parade Route - Although there is currently no parade performed regularly, the usual route for when one is performed during special events is shown in red.

slands of Adventure Map

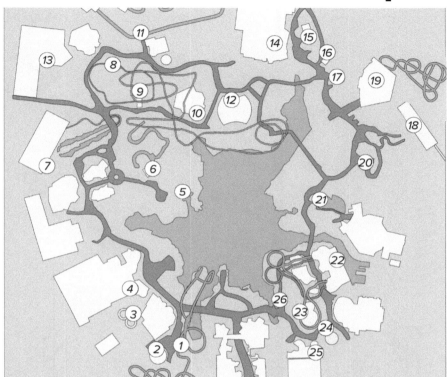

1ARVEL SUPER HERO ISLAND
. The Incredible Hulk Coaster (Express)
. Storm Force Accelatron (Express)
. Doctor Doom's Fear Fall (Express)
. The Amazing Adventures of Spider-Man
xpress)

OON LAGOON
. Me Ship, The Olive
. Popeye & Bluto's Bilge-Rat Barges
xpress)
. Dudley Do-Right's Ripsaw Falls (Express)

JRASSIC PARK
. Pteranodon Flyers
. Camp Jurassic
0. Jurassic World VelociCoaster (Express)
1. Jurassic Park River Adventure (Express)
2. Jurassic Park Discovery Center

KULL ISLAND
3. Skull Island: Reign of Kong (Express)

THE WIZARDING WORLD OF HARRY POTTER - HOGSMEADE
14. Harry Potter and the Forbidden Journey (Express)
15. Flight of the Hippogriff (Express)
16. Live Performances
17. Ollivanders
18. Hogwarts Express - Hogsmeade Station (Express)
19. Hagrid's Magical Creatures Motorbike Adventure

THE LOST CONTINENT
20. The Mystic Fountain
21. Mythos Restaurant

SEUSS LANDING
22. The High in the Sky Seuss Trolley Train Ride! (Express)
23. Caro-Seuss-El (Express)
24. One Fish, Two Fish, Red Fish, Blue Fish (Express)
25. The Cat in The Hat (Express)
26. If I Ran the Zoo

Volcano Bay Map

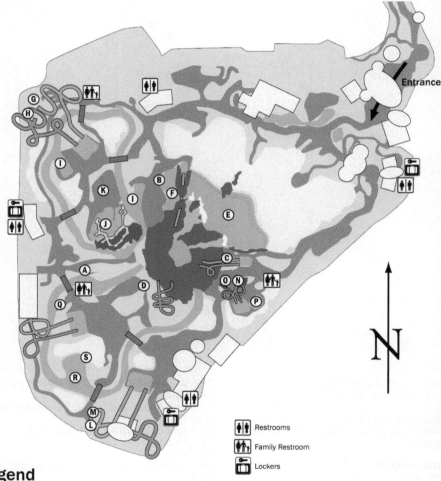

Entrance

N

Legend

KRAKATAU
A. Krakatau Aqua Coaster
B. Ko'okiri Body Plunge
C. Kala and Tai Nui Serpentine Body Slides
D. Punga Racers

WAVE VILLAGE
E. Waturi Beach
F. The Reef

RIVER VILLAGE
G. Honu
H. Ika Moana
I. Kopiko Wai Winding River

J. Runamukka Reef
K. Tot Tiki Reef

RAINFOREST VILLAGE
L. Maku
M. Puihi
N. Ohyah
O. Ohno
P. Puka Uli Lagoon
Q. Taniwha Tubes
R. TeAwa The Fearless River
S. Hammerhead Beach

Restrooms

Family Restroom

Lockers

Milton Keynes UK
Ingram Content Group UK Ltd.
UKHW021528030724
445110UK00035B/747